Exile on Main St.

Bill Janovitz

continuum
NEW YORK • LONDON

2010

The Continuum International Publishing Group Inc
80 Maiden Lane, New York, NY 10038

The Continuum International Publishing Group Ltd
The Tower Building, 11 York Road, London SE1 7NX

www.continuumbooks.com

Printed in the United States of America

Library of Congress Cataloging-in-Publication Data

Janovitz, Bill.
Exile on Main St. / Bill Janovitz.
p. cm. — (33 1/3)
Includes bibliographical references (p.   ).
ISBN 978-0-8264-1673-5 (pbk. : alk. paper)
1. Rolling Stones. 2. Jagger, Mick. Exile on Main St.
I. Title: Exile on Main Street. II. Title. III. Series.
ML421.R64J36 2005
782.42166'092'2—dc22
2004026174

Acknowledgments

Thanks to David Barker for giving me a shot, and to Chris Woodsta, Tom Erlewine, and all the folks over at Allmusic.com, where I first contributed some song reviews from *Exile on Main St*. I am very grateful for the interviews that Al Perkins, Bobby Whitlock, Graham Parker, and John Van Hamersveld granted me. Thanks also to Dominique Tarlé, whose book of photography and accompanying text, *Exile*, depicting and describing the making of the album, was a uniquely valuable source for my research. Ian McPherson's web site Time Is on Our Side (www.timeisonourside.com) was also particularly helpful in culling quotes and data. And of course, thanks to my wife Laura St. Clair and daughter Lucy for allowing me the time and providing me the support to take on the project. I also express my gratitude to Gary Smith, Joyce Linehan, Tom Johnston, Paul Kolderie, Mike O'Malley, and Mike Gent, all of whom helped this project along. And thanks to my parents, William P. and Rosemarie E. Janovitz, for their gifts of *Exile on Main St*. and my first guitar.

Also available in this series:

Forthcoming in this series:

PART I

The single greatest rock & roll record of all time,
okay? Don't send me any letters, and hold your calls.
I can almost see you holding up and waving your Beatles
records, your *Pet Sounds*, dusty old LPs in faded jackets,
worthy contenders all, I am sure. Brilliant pop records,
masterpieces even. But not the greatest, most soulful,
rock & roll record ever made. That is *Exile on Main St.*,
somehow even more glorious 30-odd years later, in its
faded and yellowed sleeve, worn-in like a baseball mitt
or torn and frayed like your favorite jeans. It is a seamless
distillation of perhaps all the essential elements of
rock & roll up to 1971, if not beyond. Not a pastiche,

mind you, but a powerful cocktail that keeps you coming back.

What is it missing? Some electronic bleeps? Early Moog sounds? Some dissonant metallic screeching, pretentious monotone vocals, and barely audible "poetry"? Yeah, I know, there is a whole plethora of new ideas that have brought rock & roll forward. Or is there? When my iPod randomly shuffles from the Stones' "Ventilator Blues" to Radiohead's "The Gloaming (Softly Open Our Mouths in the Cold)" into the Band's "Yazoo Street Scandal" (the *Music From Big Pink* outtake), and then into Howlin' Wolf's "Dorothy Mae," it all makes sense. All of these songs, spanning six different decades of pop music and three different countries, are basically blues numbers written and performed by masters. In lesser hands, the postmodern electronic percussion and noise that Radiohead uses would simply sound gratuitous. On "The Gloaming," the techniques are simply tools to add a fresh perspective, the same way the Band used Garth Hudson's otherworldly organ to haunting effect on "Yazoo Street Scandal" or Wolf's dusty growl scares us to death with its implied desperation. All are paranoid, urgent, and insistent numbers. As Mick Jagger said in 1972 regarding "electronic music," "The real experiment is what you want to say. You can express a very freaky or experimental idea in a strict framework, or you can express a very trite, boring, oft-repeated idea within an experimental framework."

The most important growth spurts in rock & roll have largely come in form, style, and presentation—shifting dynamics, instrumentation, packaging, and of course, clothes and hair. The English music press in particular (the weeklies, anyway) has always interpreted new hairstyles as indications of exciting new musical forms, and young bands continue to buy into it whole-sale. Keith Richards' greatness has never resided, Samson-like, in his self-styled hair, though it certainly adds to the allure. And the packaging of *Exile on Main St.* was designed as brilliantly as most Stones projects. But it is the music within that lasts decades later.

Don't get me wrong, I am a child of the punk rock era and many of those bands are my heroes. I also love the elements of late-70s punk rock and disco that informed the Stones' 1978 LP *Some Girls* and seemed to reenergize the band. And I totally dig the elements of Philly-soul and even the fake reggae that Jagger adopted for *Black and Blue.* Yet, though the Stones had passed through various experimental phases, they've always had songs—even when they were cover versions—that harnessed the pure emotion and raw fury of the blues and early rock & roll. The Beatles were amazingly polished and sounded like fully-hatched professionals by the time they were unleashed on the American public. By comparison, the very early Stones were amateurs— fresh, sexy, swaggering amateurs to be sure, but amateurs nevertheless. It took Andrew Loog Oldham, their manager at the time, locking Jagger and Richards in a room together to get them to compose their first original song, "Tell Me," in 1964. Or so goes the legend.

But what the Stones did have, even back then, was an undeniable attitude and an intrinsic understanding of American blues, soul, country, and rock & roll idioms. Along with many of their British Invasion colleagues, they exploded from the clubs of the 1960s with the zeal of converts. The Stones had not only studied those American records, they *got* them. And they spit them back out with authority and righteousness, adding their own flavor; they sprayed them back out at the majority of American teenagers who had not really heard these musical forms in their original, raw stages. They became blues, soul, and R&B singers, not merely copyists or thieves (unlike, say, Led Zeppelin). The Stones paid tribute to their influences musically and literally, dragging Howlin' Wolf onto the sets of pop music television shows, for example. But neither were they and their colleagues simply ambassadors; they subsequently made the music their own—almost immediately, as in the case of the Beatles. It seems to have been the attitude, the swagger, and the braggadocio of blues as much as the songs themselves that appealed to these young men. But it was the songwriting that made the Rolling Stones legends and gave them longevity, sustaining them generations beyond their teen idol phase.

By the late 60s, the Velvet Underground had been making maverick stylistic musical leaps and offering challenging lyrical conceit, and Iggy and the Stooges were ramping up the volume and showmanship, and stripping away anything else peripheral to the music. But these were just variations on what the Stones had been spinning into hits for about a decade. Perhaps those acts reminded the Stones that they were best at the primordial and that the ambitious, the Kinks-ian, satirical asides of *Between the Buttons* and the drugged-out, "we can do it too" of *Their Satanic Majesty's Request* LPs were for the most part the sorts of experiments best left to others. The Stones were never convincing at psychedelia. Even the psychedelic-era "Jumpin' Jack Flash" is the sort of quintessential blues-riff-rocking that defined the Stones. In 1972, the pre-punk energy of the Stones was still on display in the full-throttle amphetamine rush of "Rip This Joint," about as breakneck and primal as almost any version of "White Light White Heat" or "Raw Power." It was a give and take. "I mean, even *we've* been influenced by the Velvet Underground," Jagger told an interviewer in 1977. "I'll tell you exactly what we pinched from (Lou Reed) too. You know 'Stray Cat Blues?' The whole sound and the way it's paced, we pinched from the very first Velvet Underground album. You know, the sound on 'Heroin.' Honest to God, we did!"

Reed, Cale, and company were crafting epic 15-minute guitar drones and singing reportage of drugs, S&M, etcetera as early as 1966 and '67. They were all edge. This darkness—the unrefined, big repetitive guitar-riff, Bo Diddly drone, and leering vocal bluster, this blues influence—is always there in the Stones, even if it seems they have drifted at times. It might have taken the Rolling Stones until 1969 to let loose with the long-form sturm-und-drang of "Midnight Rambler," but the danger has always been present in the blues. The bleak decadence of not just the African-American blues, but also the traditional European sort explored by Brecht and Weil, Andre Gide, Thomas Mann, and others, is very much on display on *Exile*.

So even though Joe Strummer declared in 1977 "no Beatles, no Stones, no Elvis in '77," it was probably borne as much out of the frustration of a jaded fan in the face of the borderline self-parody of his erstwhile heroes and their increasing musical irrelevance as it was self-serving sloganeering for publicity, an angry young man's way to distance himself from the previous generation. In fact, an older, wiser Strummer told *Uncut* magazine in 2002, "I like every period of the Stones, really . . . "

By the late 1970s, the Stones' collective exploits, their jet-setting, bed-hopping, syringe-stabbing, powder-sniffing ways, were no longer compelling enough for many of their fans as extraneous subject matter to keep their records afloat for very long. The decadence of rock music's aristocracy was bleeding ennui into what many fans felt were half-hearted efforts. Let's not let them take the music down with them, right? Strummer's sloganeering, or at least the sentiment behind it, seemed to have some effect: the Stones fired back with their leanest and meanest record in years, *Some Girls*. And the lyrics harkened back to the torn, frayed, and tattered demon's life-sway that actually seemed inspired and, yes, urgent. It reminded people of *Sticky Fingers* and *Exile on Main St.*, early 1970s records in which the Stones were bearing witness to the promise of a generation slipping away into irrelevance, casualties dropping off, "the demon life" catching them in its sway. And then, even as they watched and warned, from the point of view of many of their fans, they succumbed, as helpless as Mick Jagger's protagonist in "Rocks Off": "I want to shout but I can hardly speak."

Exile is not the most pristine recording, but that criticism is far overplayed. If you were to talk to music producers or engineers (not that I would recommend that), you would be hard-pressed to find many who even say it sounds like a *decent* recording. "Soupy" and "swampy" are two well-used adjectives one sees when reading about the album. This is more than an exaggeration, though, and yet still such impressions of the record persist. It is not a collection of virtuoso performances. Though there are some continuous themes, it is not, as far as I can tell, a concept record. Aside from, or even in spite of, its length, *Exile* does not seem to reflect any extraordinary grandiose ambition to transcend rock and *take it to another level, man*. On the contrary, it seems to revel in self-imposed limitations. In fact, it sometimes sounds ancient. Other times, it sounds completely current and modern. It sounds, at various points, underground and a little experimental, and at others, classic, and even nostalgic.

Exile is exactly what rock & roll should sound like: a bunch of musicians playing a bunch of great songs in a room together, playing off of each other; musical communion, sounds bleeding into each other, snare drum rattling away even while not being hit, amps humming, bottles falling, feet shuffling, ghostly voices mumbling on- and off-mike, whoops of excitement, shouts of encouragement, performances without a net, masks off, urgency. It is the kind of record that goes beyond the songs themselves to create a monolithic sense of atmosphere. It conveys a sense of time and place and spirit, yet it is timeless. Its influence is still heard today. Keith Richards has said, tongue in cheek, the record "was the first grunge record."

Here is the sound of not just the Stones, but of rock & roll as a whole settling into the 1970s, as the music grew up. It's the sound of maturity, not in the sense of grown-up hippies picking up acoustic guitars and gazing inward soul-searchingly and all that, but in the sense of a once awkward and rebellious adolescent finally becoming comfortable within himself. *Oh yeah, this is what I am, should have always been, and should forever be.*

While *Exile* contains some undeniably classic songwriting and a genuine hit or two, much of the record seems filled with happy accidents and inspired spontaneity. Producer Paul Q. Kolderie (Belly; Radiohead; Pixies), who I worked with on Buffalo Tom records, was fourteen at the time of *Exile's* release. "It hit me: the look of it, the sprawling, it seemed like so much, you could just get lost in it," he told me (I ignored my own caution about talking to producers).

> It just seemed so vibey and just groovy and weird, and no rock album, to me, had sounded like that. . . . You know I was just getting a full blast of this, like, "what the fuck, this ain't the Beatles." "Tumbling Dice" that summer was coming out of every window and every

car. It was so awesome that they make a record up that was so ramshackle and so fucked up and come up with a song like that, to nail it down with—I don't know if it was number one but it was a huge hit—and such a good single and such a classic, they still play it to this day.

Though *Exile on Main St.* ended up being the key that unlocked a whole world for me, it was not my first Stones record. I had inherited from my next door neighbors some old singles: a rope (literally) of 1960s, mostly British Invasion 45s, with a few choice light-blue London label Stones sides, the twine running through the wide holes on the discs, looped and knotted and about to be put out for trash pickup. I did not have the advantage of older siblings to pass down their music to me. But that made the sense of personal discovery only more fulfilling. I also inherited a few mono Stones LPs like *Out of Our Heads* from some other neighbors. And then I went on to buy and build my own Stones collection. I think I had *Sticky Fingers*, *Let It Bleed*, certainly *Hot Rocks*, and some others before I finally attained the holy grail of *Exile*. I needed those more easily digestible single-disc LPs and greatest hits collections—each rich with actual or possible hits—before I could take on the sprawling, imposing, and impenetrable *Exile*.

By the time I was thirteen, the Stones were seemingly ubiquitous in my life: posters on my wall, popping up on my favorite show, *Saturday Night Live*, in *People* magazine at my barber (who I visited far too often for my preference). One essential cog I was missing was *Exile on Main St.*, that enigma of an album under a black and white collage, with the title and the band's name barely legible, scrawled in shaky handwriting—à la Neil Young, another hero of my early teens. The album was only a few years old at that point, but it seemed ancient. Six years is a long time when they stretch from kindergarten to sixth grade.

Somehow, on Christmas Day 1978, instead of me tearing open the gift wrapping to reveal the coveted *Exile*, it was my younger brother, Paul, who did. I was convinced this was a mistake, even though he was intent on imitating my every move at the time and might well have asked for it himself. I don't remember what kind of arguments ensued or what pleas I made to my parents. I am certain that they were as dramatic and logical as anything Oliver Wendell Holmes ever laid down ("Ladies and gentlemen of the jury, I *beseech* you . . . "). My brother, though, was pleased with the gift. He was fast becoming a rock & roll connoisseur as well. I was left to wheeling and dealing directly with him. Almost immediately, I maneuvered, planning and executing a coup, a Manhattan-from-the-natives style land grab from my younger brother that would make me look like a record-collecting Donald Trump.

Unflinchingly, I traded seven or eight of my Zeppelin records to my brother for that one Stones record. I did not think twice. At the time, it was a win-win. To this day, we both feel it was like a good baseball trade in which both sides get what they need at the time and walk away satisfied. Of course, I've since gone back and purchased copies of all those lost Zeppelin records on CD (I just listen to Plant's voice and try to ignore lines like "if there's a bustle in your hedgerow don't be alarmed now / it's just a sprinkling for the May Queen"); but all of them together will never hold a candle to the single greatest rock & roll record of all time.

I held the reward in my hands, looked over the artwork, mesmerized by the strange world it promised within. What seemed to be a chopped-up collage of circus freaks was on one side, and on the other were film frames with the faces of the Rolling Stones themselves—a none-too-subtle mirror-image juxtaposition. After all, the Stones were freakish outsiders—as long-haired threats to decency in their nascent period; as young Brits interpreting American musical idioms; then off to France as tax exiles, weary from the pressure of the English authorities. Inside, on the gatefold and individual album sleeves within, the collage continued: still shots containing 1950s-era scenes of strange Americana—dim jukeboxes, saluting veterans, more film clips of the band eating, yawning, holding up violent tabloid headlines—juxtaposed with shots of cryptic bits of lyrics, lines like "I gave you the diamonds / you gave me disease," "got to scrape the shit right off your shoes," and "I don't want to talk about Jesus / I just want to see his face."

If *Exile on Main St.* set the bar for what rock & roll should sound like, the album packaging established a standard of what it might look like: raw, enigmatic, spooky, black and white images of the band in various settings. Here is a prime example of the tragic downsizing of artwork that became inevitable as CDs edged out twelve-inch vinyl albums. Much of the concept and the photography itself comes from Robert Frank, a Swissborn émigré to the United States whose groundbreaking collection *The Americans* got right at the broken heart of America and its people—in urban and rural settings both.

Look a little closer: The "collage" on the front of Exile is actually a single shot, apparently from the wall of a New York tattoo parlor, a picture taken by Frank. The photos—some of which are featured in the *Exile on Main St.* layout—were taken on a cross-country drive in 1955 and '56 in a used car, funded in part by a Guggenheim Fellowship. The resulting book was highly influential in both form and content. If not the first, *The Americans* was one of the earliest examples of a photography book that dedicated a whole page to each photograph, with blank pages alternating opposite. The pictures are ostensibly taken in a verité style, but the results are as subjective as the most affecting works of art, particularly poetry. Frank has said, "When people look at my pictures, I want them to feel the way they do when they want to reread a line of a poem." As Jack Kerouac wrote in his introduction to the published collection, "Robert Frank, Swiss, unobtrusive, nice, with that little camera he raises and snaps with one hand he sucked a sad poem right out of America onto film, taking rank among the tragic poets of the world."

Kerouac also writes in his introduction, that the pictures remind him of "that crazy feeling in America when the sun is hot on the streets and the music comes out of a jukebox or a funeral," which dovetails nicely with *Exile on Main St.* Frank met Kerouac at a party in New York soon after the French publication of *The Americans* (an American publisher could not be secured until a year after the French publication). In photographs such as "Rooming House—Bunker Hill, Los Angeles," Frank was providing a photographic parallel to the works not just of the Beats, but echoing back to Beat predecessors like author John Fante (*Wait Until Spring, Bandini*).

It is perfect that the highly impressionistic author and poet Kerouac was chosen to pen the introduction to Frank's groundbreaking work, just as it seems so fitting that the Stones chose Frank to provide the album's artwork. Frank's is a visual—and the Stones' an aural and musical—travelogue across America and another "sad little poem right out of America." Frank's photos are deeply moving, searing their image onto the mind's retina of the viewer, particularly for an introspective suburban adolescent seeing them for the first time, freshly exposed to that "other" America that it sometimes takes an outsider's eye to see. Later, books by Diane Arbus and works by Frank's mentor Walker Evans would find their way into my hands, but I was a decidedly unworldly Long Island teenager hungry to discover what Greil Marcus later called "that old, weird, America" in his book, *Invisible Republic: Bob Dylan's Basement Tapes*.

Frank, another obvious exile, became known for his ability to virtually disappear, to blend in with his surroundings, capturing with his small camera the faces, the tiny dramas, and the surface Americana that he observed. Small things taken for granted in America fascinated him: signs, cars, clothes, attitudes. Of one incident with a sheriff who runs him out of town, he says, "We think that only happens in films."

The pictures in *The Americans* tend to concentrate on small spaces. A shot of an empty bar in Las Vegas where a boy in a loud printed shirt stares into the glow of a jukebox—which the Stones used in the *Exile* artwork—looks claustrophobic, as the daylight tries to seep in through the porthole windows of the doors while the bar seems always nocturnal by nature, fighting against the outside world. Almost everything is dimly lit, and everything is in black and white. Even the exterior shots, the facades of brick buildings, have that Edward Hopper-like melancholy light. There is an insular feeling to the book as whole, a hemmed-in quality that flies in the face of the romantic vision of an America "from sea to shining sea," with wind-swept plains of "amber waves of grain." Instead we find these small places, a gothic America of funerals, crosses, stormy moor-like hills; with characters reminiscent of "Eleanor Rigby" grasping at fleeting moments of simple happiness and human interaction, as the clock of the human condition ticks on; "lives of quiet desperation," with only photographs offering some measure of immortality to these anonymous souls. As Kerouac notes in his introduction "you end up finally not knowing any more whether a jukebox is sadder than a coffin."

In Domique Tarlé's indispensable book *Exile*—another collection of stunning photographs, taken by Tarlé while present at the *Exile on Main St.* sessions—Rolling Stones Records honcho Marshall Chess, son of Chess Records founder Leonard Chess, recalls: "Over the years with the Stones we'd allow in writers and photographers—the right ones, those who would fit in with our scene. People like Robert Frank, who Mick turned me on to after seeing his book *The Americans*. Robert became known as the father of realism because he'd become so invisible that people would do anything in front of him. We chose him to do the *Exile* cover, which he shot in Super 8."

John Van Hamersveld was gracious in sharing with me of some of the logistics in putting the *Exile on Main St.* package together. John had been a graphic artist within the rock & roll counter-culture that blossomed in Los Angeles in the mid-1960s. After designing concert posters for Pinnacle Promoters and movie posters such as his classic for the surf film *Endless Summer*, he moved into album cover art, designing the *Magical Mystery Tour* LP for the Beatles. In 1970 he created the Johnny Deco (a.k.a. "Johnny Face") poster, with a comic book-like smiling guy with prominent lips, which he feels influenced the famous Stones' "Tongue-and-Lip" logo, designed by John Pasche and Jagger, which debuted in the artwork for *Sticky Fingers* (Jagger had been photographed wearing a "Johnny Face" T-shirt earlier).

In 1971, beginning to focus more on building on his success in designing album covers, Van Hamersveld met with photographer and art director for United Artists Records, Norman Seeff, a "beatnik-like artist from Johannesburg, South Africa." Seeff had a deal with the Stones for putting together a songbook. The two got the call to come and meet with Jagger and Richards at the Bel Air villa where the Stones were staying in Los Angeles while they put the finishing touches on *Exile* at Sunset Sound. As Van Hamersveld wrote in his "Imaging the Stones" postscript to Tarlé's book:

> As I was there sitting next to Jagger, Robert Frank walks into the room with a small super eight millimeter Canon camera. I knew of him from a meeting in New York from 1968. After I left he takes Jagger to downtown Los Angeles to film him on the real seedy parts of Main Street.

Most fans know that the Rolling Stones romanticized 1950s America, much in the same way people like me respond to the Stones heyday of the '60s and '70s, and *Exile* in particular. Van Hamersveld told me that the band saw themselves as carrying the torch of not just the blues artists they emulated, but of all sorts of artists, including those associated with the Beats:

> You must understand now, Robert Frank was 50 years old in 1972, there standing in the living room of a Bel Air, Mediterranean villa, lush, and old world, they, the Stones image, of wealth, success, as pop culture post dandies, post hippies, now bluesmen looking back into the '50s, (Marshall) Chess and his connections. Frank the photographer, holding the 8mm camera, under his arm, is there now an old hipster from the '50s, as an artist from NYC. At the villa were Keith and Mick, as they outwardly, loved Frank for his con-

nections to the beat attitude, and smoking pot then with Ginsberg. They were the Beat! We seated there on the couches, we were in our thirties, the new hip, he as a father figure . . .

Jagger knew how to sell it all. He has always been a student of American pop culture in general, with a keen awareness of cutting edge artists. As with Elvis Presley before them, the Stones had already shown a well-developed ability to co-opt and make marketable the underground and raw street culture. Unlike Presley, however, who was down in the trenches, born poor in the South, Jagger was an effete upper-middle-class kid from the London suburbs, who had spent his adolescence listening to blues, soul, country, and rock & roll records. Somehow, with his earthier guitar-slinging foil, Richards, as a catalyst, he has been able to capture the essence of American roots musical forms, so much so that he transitioned quickly from a fan mimicking his idols to a genuinely adroit and influential soul singer himself. Forget the "blue-eyed" qualifier; Jagger is a great soul and blues singer in his own right. Take, for example, his performances on "Let It Loose" as a gospel-informed soul ballad, or "All Down the Line" as a flip side, a rave-up where Jagger's all-out performance might compete with similar up-tempo numbers from Otis Redding, Don Covay, or any of his Southern soul influences.

Presley, an early hero of Jagger's, was able to pull off similar feats a decade or so prior, integrating and owning his influences and thus producing something new. Yet while Presley grew up surrounded by African-American culture, Jagger had to make due with hard-to-find, second-hand sources. But like Presley, James Brown, and others, Jagger convincingly concocted a beguiling mix of simmering macho bluesman sexuality cut with a dose of androgyny—a heavier dose for Jagger than Elvis, but perhaps not as much as, say, Little Richard, another key influence on the Rolling Stones.

Is it any wonder, then, that Jagger not only understood how to sell the band musically but visually as well? He had taken the baton from ex-manager Andrew Loog Oldham, who had helped craft the Stones' early image as the Beatles' dark-horse cousins. Keith recalls being attracted to Oldham in part because, working under Brian Epstein, "he got together those very moody pictures of (the Beatles) that sold them in the first place." In taking up the reins from Oldham, Jagger was able to finesse the one-trick-pony, bad-boy image into a somewhat more mature and multi-layered "bad young jet-setting men" image—decadent rock & roll aristocrats. You know, the kind of thing he sang about on their later return to roots, "Some Girls":

Well now we're respected in society
We don't worry about the things that we used to be

We're talking heroin with the President
Yes there's a problem, sir, but it can't be bent

"Royalty's having a baby," was a refrain often heard from a sneering Keith Richards down in Nellcôte, while Mick was off with Bianca during her pregnancy, concurrent with the recording of *Exile on Main St.*

The Stones could still transmit the dirty feel of the underground outsider, even as they were becoming the biggest band in the world. They weren't Iggy and the Stooges or Lou and the Velvets; they had just outlasted the Beatles and had to prove that they were not overstaying their welcome. But the punters were dying for someone to carry it all on, to offer even a shred of meaning to all the death and darkness that accompanied the end of the 1960s and the cynical blankness that was staring down at them from the barrel of the 1970s. Van Hamersveld recalled Jagger's reaction to their layout for the cover for the record when he brought it by Sunset Sound to show to the band:

> "They'll love it!" I clearly understand what he means: "They'll" is a clear understanding of what the artist knows about his audience. This is pop visual language, the assumption, and the reflection of the sideshow of the inner business environment. The Crazy Business on display!

Frank took the Super 8 film of the band slumming down on Main Street in seedy downtown Los Angeles, the city's version of Manhattan's Bowery. Jagger told Robert Greenfield of *Rolling Stone* while they were still out in LA, Main Street is "real inner city," where "you can see pimps, knives flashing." As Frank might have done decades prior, Jagger took Frank and his movie camera and went out seeking a certain side of America: the dangerous authentic street down on Main St. Remember: Jagger told Marhall Chess that Frank was "the father of realism." The Stones were after something: an early 1970s zeitgeist.

So there, on the back cover and inner sleeves, is the band in various shots: walking down the street, under porn arcade awnings, laughing. Accompanying these shots are scrawled bits of lyrics, lines that don't even necessarily correspond with the recorded versions, and more band shots, in the repetition of the Super 8 film frames, adding an even more surreal tint, a druggy trail. Central to the back cover is a shot of Jagger, yawning. Is it weariness? Ennui? It enhances the hangover-sleepy languor of the record. But we also see "buddies" Jagger and Richards practically arm-in-arm at the microphone in the studio, warm light shining from underneath, a bottle of Old Grand Dad whiskey clutched in Jagger's hands, a can of beer in Keith's.

If there is one photograph that was singularly responsible for my rock fantasies, that made me know from an early age what I wanted to do and be, eventually leading to my tenure in a band, it was that one. Just as in all the live shots of the two of them in the classic pose, both singing at the same microphone, there seems to be a relaxed camaraderie between the two musicians. They look to be having a great time singing together. I wanted nothing more than such simple pleasure. It seems many rock & rollers feel the same. At times it seems like Aerosmith has modeled their whole image on such photos of Jagger and Richards. And in my conversation with the producer Paul Q. Kolderie, he brought the photo up as well, pointing out that the way they looked distinguished the Stones from their rootsy rock & roll peers, particularly from American bands. "The Stones seemed to be cooking up their own English brew with it all and it had to do more with the way they *looked:* the shaggy hair," explained Kolderie, recalling his perspective as an impressionable fourteen-year-old. "And that picture on *Exile* with Mick and Keith singing backup vocals—which is a picture taken in L.A., right?— with the Old Grand Dad, and you think *okay, this is the life for me, pal.* That and *Fear and Loathing in Las Vegas* ruined my life because they made it seem like the coolest thing you could do was just get as wasted as possible."

While the Stones were subscribing to a certain tradition, a variation on that trekked by Frank and Kerouac and the like, the band was also promoting their own rock & roll myth: A band of young friends in their prime, living in a big mansion on the beach in France, recording all night in the basement, chicks, drugs, and booze flowing, having a blast every night. Well, perhaps the only part mythological was the last bit. We all know about the love/hate relationship between the Glimmer Twins. When you're an adolescent, though—as I was when I was having these dreams of *Exile* rock grandeur— all you want to do is spend time with your friends. How could spending every night with them jamming be anything *but* a blast?

Well, all it took for me, when I finally got to taste a little bit of the rock & roll fantasy, was maybe one year recording and touring before that romantic notion of "a good time, all the time," as character Viv Savage so eloquently put it in *This is Spinal Tap*, was thoroughly debunked. Six or twelve weeks together, and your buddies and musical soulmates become your annoying brothers, or your college dorm roommate and his girlfriend in for the weekend: you just can't seem to escape them. And according to all accounts of the making of *Exile on Main St.*, that huge villa did start to feel awfully claustrophobic and dysfunctional at times, particularly near the end of the sessions.

And no one, *no one*, can look as "elegantly wasted" as Keith Richards, captured by the right photographer. The cheesy snapshot photos that exist from my time on the road show mostly bloated guys with eyes red not just from booze, but also bad camera flashes, sitting in front of slimy deli trays and German phallic graffiti in closets-*cum*-dressing rooms; not how I had imagined it.

After Frank clipped up frames from his Super 8 film, Van Hamersveld was in charge of putting all the pieces together. As he told me, "It seemed as if I had become the artisan arranger, a design mystic that had dropped by to give my blessing. This was the making, in a classic printmaking style of an artful image for graphic history, as myth. All the parts and pieces made sense." The postcards that came in the original album and subsequent CD re-releases were from an ill-fated photo session with Seeff (Keith was late and stumbled in the shots) that was considered for the album cover. "Make postcards," is what an unapologetic Richards told Van Hamersveld and Seeff, making an accordion-like movement with his hands. Some pens were rounded up from the Flax art store and Jagger scrawled out the incomplete credits—mistakes, oversights, and all.

The record changed from its previous working title of *Tropical Disease* to its now famous name. "We were exiles and there was a certain spirit on that album—you can throw us out but you can't get rid of us," recalled Keith Richards in a 2002 interview for *Mojo Magazine*. "Who would understand if we called it *Exile on the Rue Des Bosches*! And since 1964 or '5 we'd been spending nine months of every year in America, and a lot of the songs, the things that come out, are things you've thought about on the road. It's all American music basically—or if you want to take it all the way, it's all African." Perhaps it is obvious to point out, but Frank himself was essentially an exile on Main St., USA during his cross-country trip. The Stones clearly identified with this, though they could never be flies on the wall, not with all their fame. We can see this on display in the documentary film that Frank made of the subsequent American tour in support of *Exile*. The musicians stick out like exotic gypsies or extraterrestrials in hotel lobbies, Southern juke joints, and the like.

Looking at *Exile*, we are supposed to believe that these Riviera tax refugees spend their free time on seedy streets hanging with pimps in front of porn theaters rather than on Mediterranean beaches. And, in fact, we do buy it. We want to suspend our disbelief. And we can do so easily because the music alone is so convincing. But it is a combination of memory, fantasy, imagination, and the band's reality at the time that informs the record. As Bill Wyman details in his book *Stone Alone*, the Stones had lived and played in squalor in the early days. And Keith must still have been frequenting some shady places from time to time in the quest to feed his habit. In a *Rolling Stone* article documenting the Stones' "farewell tour" of England in 1971, Robert Greenfield describes the same sort of sleazy dressing rooms "filled with parasites" that Jagger sings about on "Torn and Frayed."

More than a decade later, when Van Hamersveld met with John (Johnny Rotten) Lydon to discuss providing the design for Public Image Limited's 1984 record *This Is What You Want*, Lydon admitted that the design of *Exile* was influential to the rough, black and white, cut-up graphic look of 1970s punk rock. It seems this influence was deeper than the mere look of the surface (scrawled writing, newspaper headlines, etc.). As Van Hamersveld recalled, Lydon also made the point that the *Exile* artwork taught the nascent punk rocker that the look of the cover art informs the overall band image and prepares the listener for what he or she is about to hear. So while the music certainly influences the decisions about how the record should look, it actually works the other way as well; the artwork informs the listener how to feel about the music it contains.

"*Exile* doesn't try anything new on the surface, but the substance is new," Van Hamersveld points out. And punk rock, especially early punk rock, was nothing really new at the base of it; it was all the same three chords and rock & roll vocals, albeit exaggerated in delivery and perhaps a bit more raw in form than most mainstream rock of the era. Lydon, and especially the Sex Pistols' manager, Malcom McClaren, had learned that it was all about packaging and marketing. John Hamersveld had learned that lesson years before as a commercial artist and through working with rock artists like the Stones. The latter were selling, or at least defining, a lifestyle for him and his peers. He recalls taking stock of the "cultural landscape" as 1970 rolled around:

> Sex, drugs, and rock n' roll has made its way into the pop language. Pop Art's look of self-conscious innocence in the early sixties has changed by the end of the decade to a slick, crafted image as a marketing tool for the record companies. (Regarding) Keith: A lot of what I'd learned at art school came home to roost. About selling a look, an attitude, an image—like what kind of hair you wanted. By the seventies the Rolling Stones Tongue-and-Lip design is the most sexual image in the media culture. Jagger's mouth and words have become a symbol and registered trademark image to be merchandised by 1971.

Anyone familiar with Keith Richards' interviews over the years, but particularly and pointedly around the time of Mick Jagger's first solo record, will be aware of how important the concept of the band is to Keith. On *Exile on Main St.*, the individual musical ego is sublimated for the good of the whole. The sum of the parts is greater. Whenever he was pitched the idea of doing a solo record, Andy Johns said Keith would brush it off. In *Keith Richards, Life as a Rolling Stone*, by Barabra

Cherone, Johns recalled that he continued to pressure Keith with the idea, after all the sing-alongs at Villa Nellcôte and then more urgently after recording "*Happy*":

> Keith started singing these cowboy songs and his voice was incredible. So I said "Goddamn, Keith, when are you gonna make an album of your songs, 'cause it's so good." And Keith sorta went, "no, man." But I kept on at him and I usually get my own way.
>
> For a month I kept on without pressuring him too much, and in the end he said, "Listen, if I made a fuckin' album of my own I'd only get all the boys to play on it anyway. So it would be a fuckin' Rolling Stones album wouldn't it? Why don't we get on with the Rolling Stones album we're doing now?" That sort of stunned me.

If there was a gang mentality, an attitude of "we're all in this together" *before* their self-imposed "exile" in France, the relationship as a group was apparently cemented during the recording of *Exile on Main St.* Which is not to say they all became one big happy family—but they were a family, albeit a slightly dysfunctional one. After the heat of all the drug busts, the death of Brian Jones, and now the tightening of the financial screws that came with being in the top tax bracket, the band felt forced from their own country, run out by the authorities. They had been at the butt-end of breathtakingly poor business decisions and exploitative contracts—the most recent, with Allen Klein, was the bad deal to end bad deals. Now they needed the help of one of Jagger's society friends, Prince Rupert Loewenstein, to figure out the pros and cons of becoming tax exiles. He recommended two years in France.

"In a way it was a great thing for the band," Richards told *Mojo* magazine. "Everybody had to look each other in the eye and say, 'All right, we'll do it in exile, in France' . . . in a way I think it was when the Stones decided, we're in this for a longer haul than anybody thought. Even ourselves."

The band members actually ended up quite dispersed, with Charlie Watts near Avignon and the newlyweds Mick and Bianca Jagger in St. Tropez—which apparently suited Bianca, who wished to keep herself distanced from the project. Bill Wyman's longtime partner during these years, Astrid Lundström, has said that up until the recording of *Exile*, the Stones and their families rarely socialized outside of the band and related activities. "The Stones only got together to work," she recalled. "But here, we were suddenly all thrown together in a foreign country, having to see more of each other." Wyman himself notes that when they first got down there, the band did indeed socialize often and by choice. "On Saturday Keith would arrive [at Wyman's place] with Anita and the kids, and there would be a few hangers-on like Ahmet Ertegun who came over from America. And then Mick would come by on his motorbike, and it was all very social, people jumping in the pool with their clothes on, things like that."

Keith, his wife Anita Pallenberg, and their son Marlon ended up in the grand 1899 *Belle Epoque* mansion, Villa Nellcôte, in Villefranche-Sur-Mer, down near Nice and Cannes. It was a tired old mansion, its glamour long ago faded, but there was a stunning view of Villefranche Harbor from its wide tiered terrace. Long owned by the Bordes shipping family, it had been used during World War II by the occupying German forces. Remnants of this time were still evident: there were swastika grates over the vents and suicide-morphine vials in the cellar (which were disposed of before Keith could find them). The driveway led up to the house through a thick and lush "jungle," which served well for the needed privacy. There was plenty of space to spread out—sixteen rooms and a private beach. "It was one of those places where you could go 'Yeah, I could live here!'" said Keith. But important to our story are the three levels of cellar that would eventually be juryrigged into a recording studio.

Keith, long-time "sixth Stone" Ian Stewart, Bill Wyman, and others made various excursions to scout out possible venues where they could record, with the Rolling Stones Mobile Studio truck parked outside. The truck, with its state of the art studio control room built in, had been used already by the Stones for some of *Sticky Fingers*.

Dominique Tarlé was a young French photographer who had befriended the Stones on previous occasions, and he ingratiated himself into the Stones scene full-time for the *Exile on Main St.* sessions, resulting in the masterpiece book *Exile*, which captures not only his jaw-dropping photos, but also a priceless oral history from various people on the scene at Nellcôte during that summer. "Keith told me that he was looking for a place where he could store all the sound equipment and possibly somewhere they could use it as well. So they started to look for a kind of theatre," Tarlé recalled. "He decided it was time to record an album and realized that maybe he was sitting on the studio, as there were three storeys of cellar underneath his house. So the Rolling Stones Mobile Unit was summoned down to Nellcôte."

Jo Bergman, who ran the band's office and acted as a liaison, says one of the reasons they ended up at Keith's house is that they feared they would never get him to some of the remote places they had been scouting. "At least we can get him down in the basement," she recalled was the dominant sentiment at the time. In his book *Rolling with the Stones*, Bill Wyman recalls, regarding the studio at Nellcôte, "we could guarantee Keith would be there."

Fans of the Stones should be thankful for Tarlé's pictures, which capture the decadence of the house, the lifestyle, if not the grand scope of the place. Like Robert Frank's photos, Tarlé's tend toward the shadowy, the insular, the intimate. He, too, is a fly on the wall in the dimly lit rooms, bottles and bongs lined up on sound baffles as players lounge and play—music and otherwise. In his foreword to the book *Exile*, Keith Richards wrote, "I realize, looking at these moments he captured, that he was part of the family, the band, in fact. He was also an exile in his own country. The quality of blending into the furniture and the fittings, I was rarely aware that he was working (WHICH *IS* RARE!)." Anita Pallenberg has claimed that the book is "like our family album."

Many of the photos have shown up before in various publications and, along with Robert Frank's photography and the overall album packaging, they add to the listener's image of the record, and aid us in envisioning the time and place so central to this legendary recording. We can see the decrepit basement, the damp on the walls. The summer heat is palpable in the shots of shirtless and barefoot musicians as they collaborate, guitars in hand, sitting at a piano, lying down on the floor with headphones on, listening to other musicians record parts right in front of them. We are with them sitting at the dining room table littered with the remnants of a meal, ashtrays full, Campari and wine bottles empty, strumming cover songs with guests like Graham Parsons and John Lennon. We see dogs, rabbits, kids, records, motorcycles, boats, chandeliers, and guitars, lots of guitars.

How could a kid not get wrapped up in these images? I am thirty-eight at the time of this writing, most of my "professional career" as a musician is behind me, and this record and these accompanying photos still make me want to pick up a guitar, call up some friends, bust open a bottle, and sing all night in the basement or at the kitchen table. This is the essence of playing music: joy, the sort of unbridled fun that makes up most of childhood and so precious little of adulthood. It is also an unfortunately small percentage of playing (and especially touring) in a professional band. As Paul Kolderie said to me, such pictures ruined our lives; on some level, we succumbed to the fantasy. Sure, there are moments of glory even for a club and theater level band like mine—we may not have always been playing to huge audiences, but man, we were touring around the world! Drinking, singing, laughing, making new friends, we went from basements and pizza to limos and *digestifs* at the Odeon (and back to basements and pizza). Believe me, we never bought into it, realizing it was all a fleeting farce, as we consciously tallied up the expenses that would be coming out of our recoupable balance at the label. But there was a part of me that always just wanted to relax and go with it, enjoy it, live like rock stars and have fun. Countless bands have been willing accomplices to ridiculously one-sided contracts for shots at this fantasy. It's how the record industry has survived for so long: the rock star myth.

Such photographs are clearly inspired snapshots taken over a long period of time—time that was doubtless also filled with tedium, frustration, fatigue, downtime, boredom, bitterness, insecurities, jealousy, and other adult-sized emotions that come with a bunch of artists and hangers-on living and working right on top of each other for months on end, with no clear schedule and dysfunctional or non-existent communication. Even the pictures that show the downtime, by the very virtue of being photos, inject a sense of import, or at least worthiness, by drawing attention to the subject. They fail to capture the outright depression and malevolence that can settle in on a homesick and hungover band stranded, for example, at a truck stop buffet on an interstate somewhere in the middle of Iowa. I mean, look at what I just wrote: even those words make it seem way more romantic than it is!

All accounts of *Exile* are heavy on the dark side, not just the relatively minor inconveniences that came with the recording. In a 1995 interview, Jagger looked back, not too fondly:

> (We were) just winging it. Staying up all night . . . Stoned on something; one thing or another. So I

don't think it was particularly pleasant. I didn't have a very good time. It was this communal thing where you don't know whether you're recording or living or having dinner; you don't know when you're gonna play, when you're gonna sing—very difficult. Too many hangers-on. I went with the flow, and the album got made. These things have a certain energy, and there's a certain flow to it, and it got impossible. Everyone was so out of it. And the engineers, the producers—all the people that were supposed to be organized—were more disorganized than anybody.

And Bill Wyman explained:

    . . . We worked every night, from 8pm to 3am, until the end of June (1971), although not everyone turned up each night. This was, for me, one of the major frustrations of this whole period. For our previous two albums we had worked well, been pretty disciplined and listened to producer Jimmy Miller. At Nellcôte things were different and it took me a while to understand why.

Wyman recounts that further distractions came when "recording in Keith's basement. had not turned out to be a guarantee of his presence. Sometimes he wouldn't come downstairs at all." And he didn't enjoy the "dull and boring" jam sessions that constituted most of the initial nights of recording. Keith and Anita's lifestyle "was becoming increasingly chaotic" and drugs were taking their toll on Keith and subsequently on the recording process. Possibly in retaliation, Mick would often not show up; perhaps being a newlywed was a further distraction, his and Bianca's wedding having just taken place on May 12. Then there was their announcement, a month later, that Bianca was expecting a baby. The two lovebirds were often jetting off for holidays in the middle of the time period set aside for recording. The tit-for-tat kept on escalating.

And even when the recording was going well, it was disorganized. Bill Wyman recalled, negatively, that Andy Johns would often be trying to record overdubs in the basement kitchen while people, dogs, and children, ate and made noise in the same room: "I remember Gram Parsons sitting in the kitchen in France one day, while we were overdubbing vocals or something. It was crazy. Someone is sitting in the kitchen overdubbing guitar and people are sitting at the table, talking, knives, forks, plates clanking. . . . It was like one of those 1960s party records in which everyone felt they should be involved."

But the main negative that he points to in the making of *Exile* was the increasing reliance on hard drugs. "Whatever people tell you about the creative relationship between hard drugs and making of rock & roll records, forget it," he writes. "They are much more a hindrance than a help." Wyman notes that Mick was very concerned about Keith and that the hard drugs were dividing the *Exile* personnel into camps—those who abused, and those who enjoyed in relative moderation or abstained altogether. The latter were often not included in the recording process and were made to feel alienated. Wyman showed up on one occasion to discover two of his bass parts re-recorded by Keith. And the new parts, Bill felt, were inferior to those he'd recorded.

But for all the problems and obstacles, the Stones could ultimately sell the rock & roll myth because they lived it. The lived all of it, the positives and the negatives. They even succeed at transforming the awful side of the lifestyle into a myth of decadent glamour. Not that Keith set out to, but is it any wonder his image influenced so many musicians to spike up their hair, take up smack, and cultivate their skin-and-bones physiques? I never even tried to pull it off, but always secretly wished I could. Others looked lame and ultimately died trying, including Johnny Thunders, never mind third- and fourth-generation wannabes like Guns N' Roses or the Black Crowes. That's why Elvis Costello's rise was such a pivotal moment for dweebs like me. (To paraphrase the quote attributed to David Lee Roth: most critics love Elvis Costello because most critics *look like* Elvis Costello.) But I still had a poster of Jagger and Richards up on my wall, at which my father would shake his head and mumble out of the corner of his mouth, "your heroes, eh?" The Glimmer Twins knew the attraction of the down and dirty street, the drugged and dangerous. "I gave you the diamonds / you gave me disease," Jagger scrawled in the album jacket. Coinciding with a famous *Rolling Stone* cover shot and interview with Keith Richards, the whole of *Exile on Main St.* offers up the sleazy glamour referred to now as junkie chic. The Stones were cementing their image and in turn, defining the prototypical image of a 1970s rock & roll band.

And much of that impression hinged around Keith's increasing prominence in the band's public image, a trend that had started gradually back around Brian Jones' death in 1969. In many ways, *Exile* is considered Keith's record: recorded at his house, more or less on his schedule, vocals down in the mix, guitars up. All accounts talk about long leisurely dinners set for double-digit guests, lasting until roughly midnight, when a vampiric Keith would beckon the musicians and crew to work. He would often disappear again for hours while, according to him, he put son Marlon to bed. Finally, he would reemerge in the wee hours ready to work again, by which point the others had usually drifted off or disappeared. But the sessions would usually last until dawn, players emerging out of the dank, dark, hot cellar into the morning daylight of the Riviera. "The days just ran into days and we didn't get any sleep," remembered Mick Taylor in *Mojo*. "I remember staggering out of the basement at six in the morning and the sunlight hitting my eyes and driving home." They were ghoulish outsiders, nocturnal vampires, exiles from the daylight.

All the different rooms and stalls in the Nellcôte house and its huge cellar were potential recording spots, resulting in a good amount of natural ambience, the kinds of sounds that lend a recording "warmth." It also led to ad-hoc experimentation. "You'd sort of jam an acoustic guitar into the corner of one of these cubicles and just start playing and you'd hear it back you'd think, 'that doesn't sound anything like what I was playing, but it sounds great,'" noted Keith. "So you started to play around with the basement itself, aiming your amplifier up at the ceiling instead of like normal." Wyman notes that his amp would be on one floor of the basement, while he would be on a different level, and that often the musicians were not in the same room together, though when they were "it was even more hot and sticky."

"I think it was a bunch of stoned musicians cooped up in a basement, trying to make a record," explained Mick Taylor. "Definitely the situation contributed to the music on a technical level—the fact that it was in a dingy basement, badly equipped. We wouldn't dream of making an album like that these days."

The band had recorded in unconventional non-studio environments before, such as Mick's home Stargroves in Newbury, England, also using the Mobile Unit. So this was not a new idea for them. But there are many considerations in recording outside of a studio, amenities taken for granted, like means of communication between the control room and the live room. Andy Johns had to run back and forth between the truck and basement to relay messages. "We would be hollering down, 'Are you ready?'" recalled Bill Wyman. Mick McKenna, the engineer in charge of the truck, said, "there was . . . a little CB microphone designed for the producer, but you could also record harmonica with it. There was also a black and white camera, but obviously these things weren't working too well then."

The Stones have always been known to record in an old school manner, with the band all in one room, even Mick singing in a hand-held mic, to record the basic tracks (drums, bass, rhythm guitar, scratch or "guide" vocal). This can be seen in such films as Jean-Luc Godard's *One Plus One*, also known as *Sympathy for the Devil*, which documents the making (not just the recording) of the song of the same name. The band often writes and collaborates on arrangements in the studio, and pity the engineer who does not have the tape machine running at all times, lest a magical take, or even a reference point, fails to get captured.

After the mid-1960s, as recording techniques became more sophisticated, the idea of singing in the same room with the other instruments and amplifiers became increasingly discouraged by most engineers, as it inevitably results in the bleeding of one instrument's sound into the microphones set up to capture the sound of other instruments. Thus, the engineers lose the level of control they seek to maintain over the sound for the rest of the work, especially the mixing, of the track. To avoid such a scenario, modern day recording technique has engineers trying to isolate each sound into isolation booths, with the drums in a "live room." The players can all be in the same room, but the amplifiers and vocalist are usually in isolation booths, with glass to peer through. The ideal for many engineers is to push up a fader on a mixing console and hear only that intended instrument. But on the majority of Stones tracks, in addition to hearing Mick Jagger's intended main lead vocal (recorded once the final take is chosen from among a variety of recordings of the same song) you can also almost always hear "ghost" tracks of his guide vocal underneath the mix. On some tracks, it sounds almost as prominent as an actual vocal "take," difficult to distinguish from the backing vocals.

In an interview with *Tape Op* magazine's Philip Stevenson, Andy Johns spoke about his goal in recording rock & roll bands:

> Stevenson: Your work has a very natural sound. It wears well. A lot of modern recordings don't. They

are too fatiguing to listen to over and over. Did you set out with a specific sound in your head that you always tried to get, or is your style more an evolved product of the way you were taught to do things?

Johns: . . . As far as the thing sounding natural I suppose it's because I've always liked rock and roll bands, so my idea, even if I've done a lot of overdubs and put a lot of things on the tracks, is really to integrate them so it sounds like you're at the best rehearsal the band ever did. Just like one big lovely noise.

Stevenson: Instruments sound like instruments and it sounds like people are playing them—

Johns: Yes! People playing as opposed to some fucking sample repeating itself over and over.

Stevenson: It's sad that some people will grow up never having heard that "people playing" sound.

Johns: Yeah, it's good for me though. It means the competition's thinning out! [laughs]

"*Exile* changed the way I thought about things," explained Johns further. "Up until that point I was extremely fast—that was one of the qualities people admired. If they could do a run through with 5 or 6 or 8 pieces and you had your sound by the end of their run through, because you never know—'they-may-never-get-it-the-same-again-and-they're-artists, and all that'—so, I was very quick, BUT *Exile* . . . actually took a year. I grew up as a person and was less intimidated by the musicians and all that, and I started taking my own sweet time a bit more after *Exile*."

Almost everything on *Exile* absolutely swings, due in large part to producer Jimmy Miller, a drummer/percussionist by training, who is widely credited with helping the Stones find their famous grooves. By the time he started work with the Stones, Miller already had some very groovy productions to his credit like "Gimme Some Lovin'" and "I'm a Man," by the Spencer Davis Group, and a whole string of classic Traffic albums. He came on board after *Their Satanic Majesty's Request*, the first record the Stones produced themselves (after Andrew Loog Oldham had been jettisoned). Miller's first production was the muscular "Jumping Jack Flash" single in 1968, which was heavy on sixteenth-note shaker percussion and unique, hard-to-identify textures wheezing in the background. This bold track heralded in a new sound for the Stones, the basis of the sound for which they are most famous: the "Stonesy" sound, with a prominent Keith Richards riff and crunchy electric guitars that almost always blend together with a percussive acoustic guitar track at varying levels of prominence. Piano tracks usually add yet another percussive element in addition to extra melodic support, and organs add at least some steady padding (filling out the empty spaces at the "bottom" of a recording)—if not outright and glorious hooks, as in the coda of "You Cant Always Get What You Want" or "I Got the Blues."

Perhaps as important as the guitars in a Miller production, shakers and tambourines add movement and groove to the relatively straightforward crisp backbeats played by Charlie Watts. In turn, with the steady beat and underlying groove being driven by the percussion, Watts is free to play inventive fills. There is a Motown influence, clearly. And there is looseness, a human element that makes the sound funky. This production template clearly influenced other groups—both those who hired Miller and those not necessarily employing him, like the Kinks' 1970 single "Lola," or the Faces on any number of tracks.

Glyn Johns, who had been an early supporter of the Stones, and their main English recording engineer since day one, recalled:

> Jagger came to me after *Satanic Majesties* and said, "We're going to get a new producer," so I said, "OK, fine." He said, "We're going to get an American." I thought, "Oh my God, that's all I need. I don't think my ego can stand having some bloody Yankee coming in here and start telling me what sort of sound to get with the Rolling Stones." So I said, "I know somebody! I know there's one in England already and he's fantastic, and he's just done the Traffic album: Jimmy Miller." And it was a remarkably good record he made, the first record he made with Traffic. I said, "He's a

really nice guy." I'd met him, he'd been in the next studio room and I said, "I'm sure he'd be fantastic." Anything but some strange, lunatic, drug addict from Los Angeles. So, Jagger actually took the bait and off he went, met Jimmy Miller and gave him the job.

Bill Wyman explained it, "I think that everybody knew that we had to get back to our roots, you know, and start over. That's why we got Jimmy Miller as a producer and came out with *Beggars Banquet* and those kinds of albums after, which was reverting back and getting more guts—which is what the Stones are all about."

This was a time that found many rock & rollers giving up the excesses of mid-to-late-1960s psychedelia and finding inspiration in the roots of rock & roll and beyond. In 1967, Bob Dylan and the group which soon became known as the Band, had retreated to the Woodstock, New York area to spend days on end recording in the basement of the Big Pink house, resulting in the much-bootlegged and eventually released *Basement Tapes.* These tracks were murky home recordings, primitive but authentic-feeling soulful takes on amalgams of public domain folk, gospel, country tunes, and archaic musical forms—coupled with lyrics influenced by old myths and folklore. This was mixed with the sound that the Band became famous for, both with and without Dylan: two keyboards, an organ and an upright piano, a guitar or two (electric and acoustic), a solid, funky, Muscle Shoals-like rhythm section, and raw layered harmonies, rarely tight, often loose. Such a sound had more to do with what the Rolling Stones had been playing earlier in their career than with what they were doing immediately before hooking up with Jimmy Miller.

The Band's leader, Robbie Robertson, articulated the formulation of the Band's sound in the liner notes to the reissue of *Music From Big Pink*:

> [With the Band] the song is becoming the thing, the mood is becoming the thing . . . there's a vibe to certain records, whether it's a Motown thing or a Sun Records thing or a Phil Spector thing. I wanted to discover the sound of The Band. So I thought, "I'm not gonna play a guitar solo on the whole record. I'm only going to play riffs." I wanted the drums to have their own character. I wanted the piano not to sound like a big Yamaha grand. I wanted it to sound like an upright piano . . . I didn't want screaming vocals. I wanted sensitive vocals where you can hear the breathing and the voices coming in . . . I like the voices coming in one at a time like the Staple Singers did . . . All these ideas came to the surface and what becomes the clear picture is that this isn't just clever. This is emotional and this is story telling. You can see this mythology.

From 1968 on, many groups and artists followed these paths back to the folk, blues, soul, and country roots of rock & roll: the Grateful Dead, the Beatles, the Byrds, Creedence Clearwater Revival, Eric Clapton, Van Morrison, and the Flying Burrito Brothers, with Gram Parsons and Chris Hillman, who melded southern soul, country, and rock into what Parsons described as "cosmic American music."

By the release of *Exile*, the Stones had long been established as a blues- and roots-based group, but Jagger—perhaps viewing the glam rock of Bowie and T. Rex (whose leader, Marc Bolan, stopped by the final sessions for *Exile* in Los Angeles), and underground sounds of the Velvets et al, as more exciting and artistically relevant—was distancing himself from the record even as the Stones were finishing up *Exile on Main St.* "This new album is fucking mad," he recalled in 1971.

> There's so many different tracks. It's very rock & roll, you know. I didn't want it to be like that. I'm the more experimental person in the group, you see I like to experiment. Not go over the same thing over and over. Since I've left England, I've had this thing I've wanted to do. I'm not against rock & roll, but I really want to experiment . . . The new album's very rock & roll and it's good. I think rock & roll is getting a bit . . . I mean, I'm very bored with rock & roll. The revival. Everyone knows what their roots are, but you've got to explore everywhere. You've got to explore the sky too.

Anita Pallenberg says, "It was also the period where Mick thought 'God what are we going to do next and how long is it going to last?' All of that was still going on."

Nevertheless, at least under the sway of Keith Richards, the Stones saw themselves as part of these traditions, getting back to their blues roots (mostly country-blues and folk) on the raw-sounding *Beggars Banquet* in 1968. Is it any wonder then that trad-blues purist Mick Taylor was installed as a replacement for the Elmore James-inspired Brian Jones?

The Stones recorded "Country Honk" in a Jimmie Rodgers style for the 1969 LP *Let it Bleed.* Their next record, *Sticky Fingers,* contained the country song "Dead Flowers," the traditional Mississippi Fred McDowell country blues "You Gotta Move," and the churchy gospel-soul of "I Got the Blues." This was the direction of the band. Country and soul melded with blues and the heavy rock & roll riffing the Stones were known for—all intensified by Jagger's self-conscious experimental leanings—leading up to *Exile on Main St.*, perhaps the finest realization of what Gram Parsons was getting at when he coined the term "cosmic American Music." And when they got to France, it seems the band was able to process such influences more consciously. Keith explained, "But by being in Europe and having had time to think about it, all of us had been picked up by working in the south of America and the people we'd met and musicians. After all, Gram Parsons was down there with us and there were loads of other musicians popping in and out."

Richards and the Stones met and hung out with Parsons and the Byrds in Los Angeles beginning in the late 1960s, while mixing *Beggar's Banquet*, and then later again when the Americans stopped in London. "Gram Parsons blew into town with the Byrds, who were playing Blasés," recalled Richards. Parsons was present for much of the summer at Nellcôte. It appears he was mainly there for inspiration and for the hang, as it seems that no one is able to place him directly on any track on *Exile*. "The reason Gram and I were together more than other musicians is because I really wanted to learn what Gram had to offer," Keith told an interviewer. "Gram was really intrigued by me and the band. Although we came from England, Gram and I shared this instinctive affinity for the real South." Parsons ended up traveling along with the Stones during their 1971 "farewell tour" of the United Kingdom and stayed at Nellcôte for most of the *Exile* sessions.

Hiring the American Jimmy Miller, then, was consistent with the Stones wanting to get back, to find the real heart of American roots music, "the real South." Miller was at the helm during what many regard as the

Stones at their untouchable peak, and Keith Richards has said that Jimmy Miller was "at the height of his talents" during *Exile on Main St.* "Nobody has really stated how important Jimmy Miller's contributions to *Exile* were," Mick Taylor told *Mojo.* " . . . A good drummer, a talented producer and our guide." Taylor pointed out how the band would often hit creative roadblocks, with songs just not coming together, and Miller often offered the solution. "I remember he actually got behind the drum kit to show Charlie how to play a particular beat." Indeed, Miller did the same on "You Can't Always Get What You Want," from *Let it Bleed.* That is Miller playing the song's shuffling beat, which Charlie never latched on to. It's a beat I don't believe Watts has ever played on subsequent live versions. And that is Jimmy Miller on the drums on *Exile*'s "Happy."

"The Rolling Stones were never great musicians," continued Taylor. "When I first joined them I couldn't believe how bad they were. I thought 'How do they make such great records?' When I met Jimmy it all fell into place. It is not about being great musicians but about a certain kind of chemistry the band has." Andy Johns has said on many occasions that when the Stones were not clicking, they were dreadful, "they could sound like the worst band on the planet. Just awful, like anti-music. But when it finally came together, it was like magic."

PART II

One of the records I owned when I was a child was a 45 I inherited from my mother, who was a big Elvis Presley fan. It was "Teddy Bear" backed with "Loving You." Since I was a kid, "Teddy Bear" obviously received a lot of spins on my portable record player. But it was really "Loving You" with which I became infatuated. Looking back, I realize how odd a song that is for a young child to focus on. Written by Brill Building legends Leiber and Stoller, it is an extremely intimate song in content, sound, and performance. It's highly charged and romantic, with a traditional Tin Pan Alley ballad structure and melody. But, in the hands of Elvis, it's a slow-burning, ultra-sexy, slow dance number. What captured me early and often, however, was the *vibe* of the record; the heavy, haunting sense of atmosphere. It feels like it was recorded at 3:30 AM. Presley sounds like he is slow dancing with a girl after all the guests have left a party or a club, the lights are low, overturned drinks and empty glasses and full ashtrays cover every surface. The piano is impossibly behind the beat. An upright bass pulses slowly, quietly, but insistently. The Jordanaires coo softly in the background. Elvis seems like he can barely raise his voice above a mumble and when he does, the results are striking and highly charged, spine-chilling. There is little evident studio compression to mess with the dramatic vocal dynamics. He sounds as if he is tipsy, drunk even, but totally in control. Presley is within the song and it is more romantic than sexual, but it could comfortably sit next to Marvin Gaye's "Sexual Healing" on a compilation disc. While I could have had little comprehension of the content of the song at such a young age, I had an instinctive awareness of the power, the undeniable force of the feeling simmering there.

There is a similarly heavy sense of atmosphere pervading *Exile on Main St.* This is no accident: Keith Richards told Stanley Booth that "the first record that really turned me on out of the rock & roll thing was 'Heartbreak Hotel,'" another song with an intrinsic sense of space. The essence of the *Exile* sound has made an everlasting impact on rock & roll production. Daniel Lanois (producer of U2, Bob Dylan, and Emmylou Harris, among others) has seemingly embraced the whole romantic idea of *Exile* for his recording philosophy. His famous studio, Kingsway, is an old house in New Orleans, and Lanois' records are deeply steeped in interesting atmospherics. Such attention to room sounds and organic textures is perhaps more appreciated in this current era and can be heard on such records as Solomon Burke's *Don't Give Up on Me*, his 2002 Joe Henry-produced comeback. Even Mick Jagger, although he feels *Exile* is "a bit overrated" and has said he feels there are only a handful of good songs on the record, told *Mojo* that "somehow, as an album, it has a great mood."

Rocks Off

What drew me in as a kid was the sound of *Exile* as a whole. The tone of the record is set within the opening seconds of the first song on side one, disc one, "Rocks Off." It begins with one of Keith Richards' trademark open G-tuned riffs. But precisely one second into it, we hear a stray bit of percussion. It sounds like someone hit a cowbell too early. Someone jumped the gun. It also sounds like a vocal microphone was left open during the mix, with some shuffling sounds before the band kicks in. This is the sort of extraneous noise that has traditionally been masked out during the mixing process, even back before computer programs like Pro Tools made automated mixing "moves" a cinch. Jagger (or whoever it is) seems all right with it, as after the first snare drum hit, we hear him growl comically "oh, yeeeeeeahhhh."

"Rocks Off" is a classic opening salvo, a shot across the bow, statement of intent—though it is by no means the only song that would be great kicking off the record; "Happy" and "All Down the Line" would work, too. But "Rocks Off" is one of the best hard-rocking songs on the record, and also one of the best of the band's deep catalog of numbers titled with a variation on the word "rock" or "rocking."

To those listening to the album upon its initial release, the buried lead vocals must have seemed a mistake. But Marshall Chess recalled, in the book *Exile*, a trick the band had learned early on from working with producer Jimmy Miller and engineers like Glynn and Andy Johns. Back in the days when AM radio was the vehicle for pop records, the mono and heavily compressed signal often exaggerated the lead vocals in a stereo mix, and they would seem like they were mixed louder than they actually were. The band found that mixing the vocals down to be a little bit more in line with the guitar tracks often resulted in an edgier and more exciting mix. For mainstream pop/rock music, *Exile on Main St.* takes that idea to the extreme, which is one element that makes the record so punk rock. The mumbles and half-heard lyrics give the album a sense of dangerous mystery, and force the listener to decipher words without the benefit of lyric sheets or explanations. Jagger obviously understood the power of this when he told *NME*, "I never like to print the lyrics. I always think that the lyrics should be listened to in the actual context of the song, rather than read as a separate piece of poetry."

Who knows what is going on lyrically in "Rocks Off"? It's another deviation on the theme of sexual frustration that started back around "Satisfaction." As with most of the songs on *Exile*, it takes repeated listenings to make out most of the words in the mix. But the ones that do jump out have that much more power, as with the famous, oh-so-Stones lyric "the sunshine bores the daylights out of me," as the song springs back to life from the helpless quicksand of the bridge. Jagger injects the line with extra punch and it's heightened by the raw harmony of Richards, yowling, warbling—my favorite kind of Keith backing track. This throat-stretching harmony is a technique he exaggerated to great effect on the band's cover of "Ain't Too Proud to Beg" on *It's Only Rock & Roll*. On *Exile*, it feels as natural as anything Keith has recorded, adding a pitch-bending twang as he slurs into the right note on the last word of the line, "me." If there is one major component missing from the Stones armory in their most recent era as rock & roll's reigning elder statesmen, it's the usurping of Keith's raw backing harmonies by polished backing singers—at least in live settings—followed, at a close second, by the replacement of Bill Wyman with jazz fusion studio bassist Darryl Jones. Not to disparage Jones, an extremely accomplished musician, but Wyman's playing is dearly missed.

Mick's narrator in "Rocks Off" might as well be one of the subjects in a dark bar in Frank's *The Americans*. He's got such playful puns throughout the record: "I'm zippin' through [or, as Jagger sings it, "zippin' chroo"] the days at lightning speed," a play on the word "speed." Keith Richards explained, "we started to reflect on what we'd seen and heard. You know, a lot of times, you're zooming through places and it takes a while for the impact to sort of settle in on you, you can't quite tell how it's going to come out on you. But, probably, what we'd done in the previous years, working through America, came out on that album."

The first lines, "I hear you talking when I'm on the street / your mouth don't move but I can hear you speak," would be spooky if they weren't sung with such playful irreverence. They are arresting, nevertheless. These are the lines that open the album, and Jagger purrs them as if he's just waking up. "Kick me like you kicked before / I can't even feel the pain no more," he yowls later, finally roused. We are not sure if we are awake or dreaming, stoned or sober. Here is Mick, in his street-wise opium dreams, a burlesque neo-Oscar Wilde, tossing off lines like "I was making love last night / to a dancer friend of mine / I can't seem to stay in step / 'cause she come every time she pirouettes for me." He awakes as if into some sort of hangover from a sexual ennui cocktail. Perhaps with the "sunshine" and not feeling "the pain no more" lines, Jagger is also giving voice to a Keith Richards character, as he so often does on the album. Maybe Keith even fed in these lines during the collaboration. The lyrics of *Exile on Main St.* are as essential in painting the picture of this being "Keith's record" as any other component of this guitar-driven, back-to-basics rock album recorded in his house. We have the guitar player of "Torn and Frayed"; we have the "Berber jewelry jangling down the street" in "Shine a Light"; we have the Keith signature anthem of "Happy."

On "Rocks Off," the main riff almost instantly becomes two parts, one on each stereo side, both played by Richards, the second keeping a more straightforward eighth-note chugging pattern. One of the guitar tracks adds a Henry Mancini "Peter Gunn" (or "Brand New Cadillac," or "Planet Claire") kind of rhythm. But then we notice some other odd/happy-sounding third guitar part, most likely played by Mick Taylor, also rather Latin-esque, warbling as if through a Leslie organ speaker rotating at high speed. This part is set way in the background and up the center of the stereo spread. It's almost like a piano or organ in its texture.

The making of "Rocks Off" was typical of many of *Exile's* tracks, as it hinged upon the rhythms—circadian and musical—of the band, and of Keith's muse in particular. The basic tracks were apparently laid down quickly in an all-night session, everyone heading off to bed around dawn, including engineer Andy Johns. Johns told Steve Appleford, in *Rolling Stones Rip This Joint: The Stories Behind Every Song*, that he took this as a sign of the session's end:

> But once he arrived at the villa he shared with trumpet-player Jim Price a half-hour drive away, the telephone was ringing. It was Keith. "Where the fuck are you?" Well, you were asleep," Johns replied . . . Normally, Richards would have been inclined to wait until the next night's session. What was the hurry? But Keith was ready . . . and wasn't about to let this moment to pass. "Oh, man, I've got to do this guitar part," he said. "Come Back!"

So after Johns returned, sure enough Richards recorded the second guitar part, "and the whole thing just came to light, and really started grooving," recalled Johns.

Repeated plays offer continued revelations from *Exile*. As you become more familiar with the record, the immediate surface elements start to give way, so that "buried" parts jump out like new discoveries, as if they were recently overdubbed on a record you've listened to for decades. This phenomenon is especially acute for recording musicians, whose ears continue to develop with studio experience. Musicians become more adept at distinguishing sonic textures—specific tracks and recording techniques. Keith's subtle dueling rhythm guitar parts on "Rocks Off" are a perfect example of this.

In his original review of the album for *Rolling Stone* magazine, Lenny Kaye (later of the legendary Patti Smith Group) bemoaned the relative dearth of classic Keith riffs, the sort he had been pumping out with regularity. And yet the album has some textbook examples, like "Happy" and "Tumbling Dice." Nevertheless, the beauty of *Exile on Main St.* has proven to be in the ensemble approach of the record, with very few actual spotlight solo moments for anyone in particular.

As John Perry points out in *Classic Rock Albums: Exile on Main St.* (Schirmer Books, 1999), his informative book about the record, the horn section had "become regular members of the touring band in 1970 . . . What the Stones were approaching at this point was something new, an approach to hard rock that was entirely modern yet rooted in 1950s rock & roll and 1930s–1940s swing."

The Stones were at their peak as a live band in the early 1970s, and when they got off the road from the 1971 tour, Perry notes, "that energy carried over into the summer when work began on the new album." According to Dominique Tarlé, Richards stated, going into the recording of *Exile*, "we're really an eight piece band now."

As soon as Jagger has gotten out the second line of lyrics, that third guitar part has all but been commandeered by the first appearance of the formidable right hand of pianist Nicky Hopkins—who, on *Exile*, offers the finest performances of his tenure with the Stones, if not his career—and then the rest of the ensemble falls in with a dense yet still somehow lean rock arrangement. Hopkins hammers away eighth-note figures with his right hand, to help keep the train chugging, while also adding some amazing runs and fills.

Hopkins, who died in 1994, is an absolute animal on *Exile*, a stone virtuoso. He went back with the Stones almost to the beginning. In *Rolling with the Stones*, Bill Wyman notes that the Stones had in fact opened up for Nicky, as a keyboardist with Cyril's [Davies] All Stars in 1963. In many ways, *Exile* is the album on which Hopkins shines the most. At any given time, his piano tracks are as prominent as any instrument or vocal track on the record—and they're one of the best rewards that come from repeat listens.

Glyn Johns has said, "Nicky Hopkins was an absolute genius. I have never heard anyone play like him before or since . . . He was a sweetheart of a guy." Glyn brought him in to play on some Stones sessions after employing him for recordings by the Who and the Kinks. The Stones needed someone other than Ian Stewart, after he refused to play anything but the blues and boogie-woogie. Anything else was, to him, "Chinese chords."

I have always wondered what Hopkins was like to work with, and would have loved to have him add something to records of which I've been a part. Over the years, I've been lucky enough to meet and play with a few heroes of mine. It has been perhaps one of the best parts of being in a "professional" band on a major label. I got to make a record and tour with Graham Parker, a tour that also included Kate Pierson of the B-52s, which was like rock & roll fantasy camp. Graham made a record called *Up Escalator* (1980) and enlisted Nicky for it, as well as for the album *Another Grey Area* (1982).

"Nicky was a nice, down to earth guy, and got into the material quickly," Graham told me.

> Unlike the Rumour, who seemed always to be trying to re-arrange my songs before they'd got to know them, Nicky only had to hear a tune once or twice to memorize it. He'd listen to my suggestions and incorporate his ideas seamlessly. He had a surprisingly gentle touch on the piano; I expected a more thumping

approach, which *Exile* seemed—at least in my memory of it at the time—to suggest. But he never played anything at all with a hard attack. At one point, I even asked him if he'd play a certain number with more aggression. He kind of agreed but kept on playing exactly the same way!

Nicky said it was pretty chaotic making *Exile*. People were all over the place, in different rooms, recording bits and pieces. And of course, everyone was out of their heads from morning till morning. From what I can gather, a Stones album is not exactly put together like military operation. Nothing happens for days, then they start on something at 3 in the morning! Sounds like a nightmare to me.

On "Rocks Off," Hopkins helps to build tension at just the right times with runs up the scales. He plays the Professor Longhair and Jerry Lee Lewis boogie, jumping octaves, jabbing and weaving, fitting in between horn lines, guitar parts, vocal ad-libs. His playing is never gratuitous, and is as driving as the guitars. The piano adds that Jimmy Johnson/Chuck Berry vibe, a good old rock & roll feel. His playing is urgent but never in the way.

Hopkins' piano, as with much of the instrumentation on "Rocks Off," gives way to a concise and blistering blues lead from Mick Taylor just as the song begins its fade out. It is not so much that the horns, piano, guitars, etcetera, drift away individually; the whole song fades together, except for this amazing little lead run that seems to stay at the same level—the record revealing one of its interesting textures. It's a result of the mixing process. In the sound of the lead guitar run, you can hear an example of the room-sound atmospherics of the record. It doesn't sound close-miked at all, which would result in a more direct and cutting guitar sound; it sounds more natural than that, as if we are simply in the room listening to Taylor play his inspired run.

This small glimmer of a solo is an example of how the album's mix works. The philosophy is consistent with the great bluegrass groups, jazz combos, and gospel quartets like the aforementioned Staple Singers and the Soul Stirrers (the group that launched the career of the teenage Sam Cooke). Many of those groups recorded with only one or a few microphones in the pre–1960s recording situations. We hear blended ensembles in all those cases, with a soloist featured at times, coming more into prominence in the call-and-response tradition of the church.

And have horns ever sounded better than this on a recording? Jim Price (trumpet) and Bobby Keys (sax)—the "Texas Horns"—like Hopkins, also make the case that they are a big part of the "greatest rock & roll band in the world," not mere session men. Too often, songs have been written, arranged, and recorded by the time session musicians are hired to overdub specific parts on specific songs. Much of the time, they are handed charts and arrangements to follow. They come in, play their parts, are paid (or submit invoices), and split. And the Stones used plenty of traditional session musicians, even on *Exile*, when they went to Los Angeles for over-dubbing and mixing. In the case of Price and Keys, however, they were—at least during this era—essential cogs in the Stones machine.

Keys and Price were at Nellcôte virtually the whole time. They had their young families with them. As this record was recorded piecemeal, in spurts of inspiration, they had to be ready every night, which translated into a lot of downtime. There were many gambling excursions up to Monte Carlo, as well as simple trips to the beach and to village bars. But when the red light went on, and someone yelled down to them, the horn players would lay down celebrated parts while recording in some of the most inspired and improvised spaces imaginable: long basement corridors with high ceilings, taking advantage of that natural reverb; the cellar kitchen; lying on their backs—whichever new experiment was chosen for that night. And like all the other players in the Stones' orbit, the horn players seemed to be given leeway to come up with their own ideas for parts—often, in fact, steering the track in new directions as result—though rarely, if ever, receiving writing or arranging credit.

Price and Keys, both of whom featured heavily in the sound of *Sticky Fingers*, also played on some of those specific aforementioned generation-defining records—with Delaney and Bonnie, George Harrison, Joe Cocker, and Dr. John. The Stones first met Bobby Keys on one of their early tour stops at a state fair in Texas. Keys was a young, hell-raising Texas teen playing behind legends like Buddy Holly and—at the time the Stones met him—Bobby Vee. Keys' lifestyle choices made him a perfect buddy for Keith: "It's a gas not to be so insulated and play with some more people, especially people like Bobby, man, who sort of on top of being born at the same time of day and the same everything as me has been playing on the road, man, since '56, '57," Richards told Robert Greenfield in *Rolling Stone* in 1971, during the *Exile* sessions. "He was on Buddy Holly's first record. I mean he's a fantastic cat to know for someone who is into playing rock & roll because it's been an unending chain for him. The first few years he was playing around, man, I was just the same as anyone, I was just listening to it and digging it, and wondering where it came from. And there he was, man. Bobby's like one of those things that goes all the way through that whole thing, sails right through it."

This desire to be as close as possible to the source has always been important to the Stones, and to Keith in particular. Whether it was going to Chess Studios in Chicago on their earliest tours through America, jamming with Howlin' Wolf and Muddy Waters, tracking down Chuck Berry, bringing in Keys, Billy Preston, or inviting Gram Parsons for an extended stay at Nellcôte, these moves were all part of the musical education of Keith Richards, and added to the depth of authenticity of the Stones' take on American musical idioms.

And, as we saw in the film *Gimme Shelter*, the Stax Records-/Memphis soul-loving Stones made a pilgrimage to Muscle Shoals Sound Studios in Florence, Alabama (the outgrowth of Rick Hall's Fame Studio in Muscle Shoals), to capture some of that Southern soul sound, at the very source where white musicians and black musicians collaborated on so many soul classics by the likes of Aretha Franklin, Wilson Pickett, and Arthur Alexander, with producers like Jerry Wexler and Tom Dowd. The Stones had already covered "You Better Move On," one of the earliest Muscle Shoals-identified hits, by the now-legendary Alexander. This is where they recorded "Wild Horses," and they also apparently ran through an unrecorded version of "Loving Cup."

The musicians who made up the Muscle Shoals house band are legends among other musicians. They included Chips Moman on guitar, Tommy Cogbill on bass, Spooner Oldham on electric piano and organ, and

Roger Hawkins, who Atlantic honcho and producer Wexler called "the greatest drummer in the world—still." Hawkins' style is certainly echoed in the elegant and sublime simplicity of Charlie Watts' own drumming. Prior to the success of the Allman Brothers, Duane Allman played some solos on sessions by Aretha and Wilson Pickett in Muscle Shoals. Importantly, however, Peter Guralnick points out, "much like Stax, Fame had no flashy lead guitarist in their studio group; rhythm was the key component."

This was an underappreciated attribute when I was first learning the guitar as a young adolescent. I remember arguing on the school bus for the Keith Richards and Pete Townsend rhythm-first philosophy over the noodly wanking of those musicians primarily labeled as "lead" guitarists. The notion of there being a "lead" anything in a good band always seemed to miss the point for me. A great band fires on all cylinders, meshing, weaving, collaborating like a team, as the Stones do on *Exile on Main St.* Even a lyrical soloist such as Mick Taylor is best showcased in a song-oriented, rhythm-centered band like the Stones, far more than in a combo that spends inordinate amounts of time tediously trading solos, like some of the more traditionalist blues-based groups that featured Taylor.

On "Rocks Off," the arrangement Keys and Price play is an authoritative blast, supporting the rock & roll rhythm section, never in the way, though not shying away from leaving their mark. The horn chart is another hook, rocking as hard as any guitar. The band members all seem to feed off one another. Whether or not the horns were there for the basic tracking, or overdubbed soon after a take was in the can, they are right in the thick of it all, moving with the band in a common direction, particularly at the vamp at the end of the song. Everyone seems to be hammering away with purpose. Listen to the section between 3:34 and 3:40 for some of the most glorious give and take, an ecstatic climax to the song.

Coming in at 2:12, the minor-key bridge of "Rocks Off" incorporates elements of the psychedelic era, specifically in the backward tracking of vocals, as Jagger's and Richards' vocals swirl in upward vortexes, like ghouls sweeping up from the graves in a Halloween cartoon. The rest of the musical backing track comes out of a chorus and to a puttering halt. Charlie taps out time on the high-hat cymbals, hitting snare drum shots in a sparse new pattern, while Mick hits the tambourine. The guitars are no longer straight forward and chugging, but rather awash in a slow Leslie-speaker or phase shifter modulating effect. The dream imagery continues, musically and lyrically, as if the singer has been drawn back into sleep, fighting against the helplessness he finds in a dream: "feel so hypnotized, can't describe the scene / feel so mesmerized, all that inside . . . "

Charlie dives in full bore on the vamp/coda (end) of "Rocks Off," with a number of staggering fills. Listen to the four bar-long fill around 3:33–3:40 for an example. Charlie sounds like he is answering the horn stabs and right-hand piano of Hopkins. The guitars, drums, and percussion hold the fort down while horns slur, Jagger drawls, and a bunch of backing vocal tracks from Richards and Jagger slip and slide all over the place, rarely crisp or on the beat. But closer listening reveals a tight pattern in the chorus backing vocals, punctuating and moving the chorus along with yet another percussive element: "only *get* 'em off, only *get* 'em off, *g*et 'em off." All the vocal parts sound spontaneous and inspired, passionate, as if this is their last chance to sing them. And this, amazingly, is still the first track on the record.

Rip This Joint

Though *Exile on Main St.* eventually sprawls out stylistically over the course of its four vinyl sides, it begins with a mean one-two punch. We barely have any time to recover from the leading track before we're hit with the blistering assault of "Rip This Joint." With the boys springing from the musty basement as if with mouthfuls of trucker speed, riding shotgun in this punk-paced song that almost serves as an overture for the whole runaway train of a record—announcing stops in "Alabam'," Santa Fe, Dallas, Texas, New Orleans, even Washington, stopping to see "Dick and Pat down in old D.C."—the song takes off at a breakneck pace and never looks back. Keith Richards claimed it "was the fastest song [tempo] we ever cut."

If the sound of suburban hardcore punk ten or fifteen years later had not gotten so rhythmically rigid and straight (and straight-edge) as to all but abandon the swinging roots of rock & roll, it might have sounded something like "Rip This Joint." The Stones achieve a pre-punk energy, coupled with a sexy 1950s groove, years before punk-informed neo-rockabilly artists had any baby curls to grease down with Royal Crown. The song has the early, regional underground rockabilly flare of 1950s West Virginia wildman Hasil Adkins, who Cub Koda called "a true rock & roll primitive." And it is this sort of spirit, ripped from the raw, minimalist source, that the Stones channel explosively on "Rip This Joint."

Jagger's amphetamine rush of words is most obviously an homage to early rock & roll travelogue numbers like "Route 66" and Chuck Berry's "Back in the U.S.A." and "Sweet Little 16," though updated with the jet-set cheekiness that would later be on full display in

"Respectable." Over the walking bass line (actually, it doesn't walk, it runs) of upright bassist Bill Plummer, in place of Bill Wyman (surprising, since Wyman loves this sort of rock & roll-purist number), Richards' relentless hammering guitar, and the pounding drumming of Charlie Watts, Jagger starts off the song with "Momma says 'yes,' poppa says 'no' / make up your mind 'cause I gotta go / gonna raise hell at the union hall / drive myself right over the wall." After a couple of throaty rebel yells, his more urbane and audacious self returns, with "Dick and Pat in old D.C. / well, they're gonna hold some shit for me." Jagger has the cheek to insert this latter insolent aside after a couple of lines in which he sarcastically humbles himself, the artist in exile, to ask "Mister President, Mister immigration man / let me in, sweetie, to your fair land."

Such lines should have made "Rip This Joint" the perfect opening song for the 1972 Stones Touring Party and/or the films documenting it. Jagger gives calls out to New Orleans, with "Dixie Dean" and "Dallas, Texas, with the Butter Queen," while warning "Little Rock, and I'm fit to pop," and "Alabam' don't give a damn." Dixie Dean sounds like a New Orleans figure, and that was probably the reason he slipped into the lyrics, but it's most likely a reference to the legendary 1920s English footballer. Barbara, the Butter Queen was apparently the same sort of creative groupie as Cynthia Plaster

Caster, for, according to Keith (who recalls more than one Butter Queen) "they did loads of wonderful things with butter, apparently. I used to see them around all the time, but they never buttered me up. I used to avoid them like the plague. Anything that smacked of professionalism." In notes for the *Gimme Shelter* DVD, Stones assistant Jo Bergman recalled answering a motel door in Texas during the 1969 tour, when "a blonde with straggly hair announced 'I've got a pound of butter in my purse. Where's Mick?' She was the Dallas Butter Queen. Groupies had titles then."

Little Richard is the primary influence for "Rip This Joint." The song more or less quotes Richard's "Rip It Up," and not just its title. In the song, written by Robert A. Blackwell and John S. Marascaico, Richard sings, "I've got me a date and I won't be late / Pick her up in my 88 / trek on down to the union hall / when the joint starts jumpin' I'll have a ball." Charlie Watts says, "Richard, for me, is a very underrated person in that he really is a wonderful singer and piano player. He's fabulous. But because he's entertaining, which is what people loved about him, his playing is overshadowed by all that." Indeed, the Stones' generation might have been the last to understand the significance of Little Richard's contributions to the foundation of rock & roll—and even then, it was only the musicians who cared enough to be aware. Little Richard was in and out of retirement (to the Cloth) at this point, and in subsequent years, he slipped further into caricature and self-parody.

While "Rip This Joint" swings like the boogie-woogie piano-driven music of Jerry Lee Lewis and Little Richard, the Stones amp up the Chuck Berry guitar and piano boogie to hard-rock level. Charlie Watts tosses off efficient tom-tom rolls like Berry drummers Ebby Hardy and Odie Payne, and Nicky Hopkins channels Johnny Johnson in his piano figures. Additionally, they quote one of the lesser-known Berry titles, "Let it Rock." Jagger seems to be pushed by the band and also to be goading them on. It would be hard to picture the musicians swirling up such a storm without the vocal encouragement of Jagger, most likely in a guide vocal. His final take sounds unrestrained, as if he's whooping it up between swigs from a bottle of Wild Turkey. His singing here is like Little Richard at his most raw.

Everyone in the octet plays his heart out, trying to keep up with the others. In a caption for a picture of a wiped-out Richards lying on a mattress, Dominique Tarlé notes, "Keith played it all night long, for days. He was exhausted. It was very difficult to keep the perfect rhythm, and Jimmy Miller wanted it to be spot on. Keith gave it everything he had," trying to nail down the rapid-fire guitar part. Bobby Keys plays baritone and tenor sax, with a couple of squealing solos on the tenor, while Jim Price, on the trumpet and trombone, punctuates lines along with Keys. Mick Taylor slips in some slide parts. Plummer, a jazz player brought in by Jim Keltner, overdubbed his parts in Los Angeles during the final mixing sessions, and his slapping-style upright adds an authentic 1950s flavor. Nicky Hopkins plays the sort of boogie-woogie part normally reserved for Stones stalwart traditionalist Ian Stewart. And Hopkins is a force to be reckoned with, playing the high octaves almost exclusively in seventh chord triplets. The song is over, as if in a blur, in a little over two minutes.

Mirroring many of the subjects in Robert Frank's *The Americans*, *Exile on Main St.* often betrays a sense of weariness. This was, after all, a band that had been through an awful lot in the years leading up to *Exile*: births, deaths, arrests, marriages, break-ups, drug abuse, financial turmoil, and the constant pressure of maintaining a successful band and business. And America was beaten down by the end of the 1960s as well. But as with Frank's book, there are glimmers of not just optimism, but also the sort of outright exuberance that led Kerouac to describe Frank's work as akin to "that crazy feeling in America when the sun is hot on the streets and the music comes out of a jukebox or a funeral." If we were in New Orleans—mythical New Orleans—it would not matter which source it came from; it would be party time nevertheless. Like Frank, Tarlé captures the weariness and joy, as well as all the emotional shades of gray in between, of the *Exile* sessions.

Criticism of *Exile* as overly sprawling misses the point. Certainly the album is ambitious in its attempt to capture the breadth and scope of American music, at least the strains that appealed to the band. Though the Rolling Stones most likely did not sit down and preconceive it as such, the record seems to set out to cover nothing less than the wide-open spaces and shadowy corners of America itself via the nation's music—from urban soul to down-home country to New Orleans jazz: a musical accompaniment for Frank's photos. "Rip This Joint" sets the tone for this journey, as a modern-day "Route 66" travelogue from Birmingham to San Diego. It's as if the band had reached a tipping point, where the collective intake of influences—via the eyes and ears of all the individual members—gushed forth in a torrent, laying out a roadmap of where American popular music had been, and also where it was going: all captured on two pieces of vinyl.

Shake Your Hips

If so inclined, you can break down the songs on *Exile* into a few categories: full-tilt rockers, gospel-informed torch ballads, acoustic folk and country numbers, or bluesy grinders like "Ventilator Blues," "Casino

Boogie," "Turd on the Run," and Slim Harpo's "Shake Your Hips." The latter songs find droning grooves, churning away in the middle register, and build in intensity mostly by sheer virtue of performance over arrangement—particularly via vocal inflection and emotional resonance.

Louisiana's Slim Harpo—born James Isaac Moore—was already known to Stones fans, as he was to followers of the Kinks and Van Morrison, both of whom had covered his songs. He wrote the early Stones favorite "I'm a King Bee." Though Harpo might have taken some cues from Jimmy Reed in the lazy, leering vocal department, Slim had a more distinct country-western twang to his inflections. And he seemed to be less beholden to a twelve-bar structure in his songwriting than some other modern blues writers. He was more country than city-blues. His songs are encompassed by a distinctive mood and sound: a swampy drone that worms into your consciousness and attacks you from a different angle than a straight-on song.

Jagger affects a particular Slim-style southern accent on "Shake Your Hips," nice and loose on the behind-the-beat falsetto "now ain't that easy?"—sung as "eeeeeeeeasy," in a slippery howl almost as haunting as Robert Johnson's. It is the sort of howl that Jeffery Lee Pierce found so eerily effective as he moaned on the classic blues-punk Gun Club records in the early-to-mid-1980s.

After the dual sax and blues harp solo in the middle of the "Shake Your Hips," Jagger comes back in, his voice quivering on the verse with "met a girl in a country town," and then breaking on the refrain "SHAKE your hips, baby! SHAKE your hips, baby!" The intensity gets ratcheted up in the last chorus. Charlie plays mostly rolls on the side of a drum, while pedaling his high-hat and adding an inspired rim shot here and there. This is one of the few songs that feature Ian Stewart on piano, and it sounds like Keith takes the guitar solo here. Bobby Keys plays during the whole song, doubling the main guitar riff, which plays call-and-response with Jagger's entreaties in the chorus.

Mood and overall feel is important to the pacing and tone of *Exile*. This album is not concerned with serving up an endless parade of singles, but rather it is a collection that offers the opportunity to throw in a well-executed cover like this one to establish the vibe. Indeed, had many of these songs been buried in the middle of a later record like *Goats Head Soup*, they might have been lost and forgotten. And while they may not exactly stand out much here either, songs like "Shake Your Hips," "Casino Boogie," and "Stop Breaking Down" do find a home in the context of *Exile*, an album that works as a piece, wherein such songs are appropriated the attention they deserve, as pieces of a whole. Many fans, along with the Stones themselves, see *Sticky Fingers* and *Exile* as almost a continuous project. But with songs like "Shake Your Hips" and "Sweet Virginia," the band seems to leapfrog back a bit to *Beggar's Banquet* and pick up on some ideas started there. They take some of that record's stark country and blues bleakness and give it a bit more ground to spread out, even adding almost pure mood/sound pieces like "Just Want to See His Face."

If nothing else, on such cover versions the Stones solidify their roots and their musicianship, displaying an authoritative air of authenticity and a comfort in the blues vernacular. "You don't want to touch other people's stuff unless you've got something different to add to it, which I think we've got," noted Keith.

Casino Boogie

Has anybody been as good at making an entrance as Charlie Watts? Fashionably late, but steady throughout, Charlie tumbles in for real on the toms after slapping a creative beat on the high hat to keep time. And Keith makes it all possible by crawling out on a limb, with extreme confidence that his rhythmic riffing will be picked up and made exponentially more effective once

Charlie joins in and sets the pace for the rest of the band. This is the reciprocal energy of a band at the peak of its game—Keith sets down the groove, but can crawl as far out on the limb as he likes, because Charlie is going to be there with the footing he needs.

Continuing the drone of "Shake Your Hips," "Casino Boogie" is all mid-range: the melody is sung with just a few choice notes, with the harmony not spreading out much either; open-tuned slide and hammering guitars are added by Mick Taylor and Keith; and an electric piano from Nicky Hopkins is a part which hints at the Clavinet sounds the band would later use on songs like "Doo Doo Doo Doo Doo (Heartbreaker)." Before you even realize he's soloing, Bobby Keys emerges from a full eight bars hanging on the same two notes (mostly just one, really, with the other coming every three or four notes), busting out into more melodic phrasing for the last four bars. Keys takes a cue from jazz players like Miles Davis, or from the simple rhythmic figures that Chuck Berry would play. Melodic range is eschewed for almost pure rhythm. The tension is almost overwhelming. The band does not give in behind Bobby; they just stay in the same steady groove. You hang there with Keys on his one-note samba, waiting for release. The sexual undertone is palpable. And when Taylor takes over on the next break, he offers only a note or two more, along with Hopkins hammering on the same two-fingered chords as the arrangement fades out on the same chord. The blues of John Lee Hooker and the Chess guys are touch-points here. The music buzzes on and threatens to take the sort of malevolent turn in tone and (double) time that "Midnight Rambler" does. Instead it simply stays put, increasing in intensity, Charlie switching to the ride cymbal, as someone clanks on a bottle or can in the background.

The lyrics are an impressionistic mix of dreamy film noir:

> *Wounded lover, got no time on hand*
> *Dietrich movies, close up boogies . . .*
> *Watch that hat in black . . .*

And casual disdain for authority, drug-bust martyrdom, and the band's pressure to "exile" themselves:

> *Thrill freak, Uncle Sam*
> *All for business, no, you understand?*
> *Judge and jury walk out hand in hand . . .*
>
> *Sinking in the sand*
> *Fade out freedom, stand that heat on*

And then with two simple lines, Jagger captures the essence of *Exile on Main St.*: surreal rock & roll, jet-set sexuality, decadence, and boredom with the tired themes of the 1960s.

> *Kissing cunt in Cannes*
> *Protest music, million dollar sad . . .*

Even when adding their own contribution to 1960s protest music, the Stones' lyrics made less of a statement than did their music. Perhaps this is a truth of all great "protest" music. Like Guthrie, Dylan, the Clash, or Elvis Costello with a song like "Oliver's Army," you need to hook me first with the music and then let me figure out the message. "Gimme Shelter" is another good example, its message writ broadly, wisely. "War, children, is just a shot away" is, after all, not quite Dylan. And as with that song, it is usually the tense and/or ominous music that makes the impact.

On "Casino Boogie" the Stones are playing almost straight-up American blues, but rather than trying to hide it, they embrace the themes most relevant to their "million dollar sad" lifestyle: an almost new aristocratic decadence that would seem antithetical to what rock & roll was supposed to be—street, rebellious, dangerous. Nevertheless, they obviously felt the need to push the porn-rock envelope in order to nurture their "dangerous" image. So, this being the era when Jagger came up with the Hubert Selby-like hustler-raunch of the song "Cocksucker Blues" to satisfy a record contract, the Stones figured they should just keep testing the limits of obscenity laws—a path they continued on with "Star Star" (or its previous title "Star Fucker") and "Some Girls." Here on "Casino Boogie" they sing about living as oversexed high rollers who pass the time at the casinos at Monte Carlo, just up the coast from Villefranche, not far from the villa that Andy Johns shared with Jim Price.

Speaking about *Exile on Main St.*, Jagger has said, "there's a lot of songs that are really, like, not songs at all. Like 'Casino Boogie.' They're really nicely played, but there's no hooks in them and there's no memorable lyrics." Jagger continues to show a befuddlement with why so many fans are taken by the record. It's as if he needs epigrammatic lyrics like "you can't always get what you want" and "I can't get no satisfaction" in order to consider a song "memorable." But such lines as "million dollar sad" and "judge and jury walk out hand in hand" are indeed memorable, as is the deft irony contained therein. No one is going to mistake "Casino Boogie" for a hit song, never mind give it a place among the classic Stones pantheon. But even with an ostensibly tossed-off number like this, they don't need to do much selling at all. Jagger sings the words with power, and Keith's backing harmony is sung with equal force, giving the song an undeniable authority that transcends any question of them being white-blues-band copyists. Compare it to something like the mediocre "Silver Train" or "Luxury" of their releases in the years immediately following *Exile*. "Casino Boogie" is authoritative and muscular. The recording sounds effortless.

Tumbling Dice

A lot of pop music is inherently nostalgic, but the Stones had been around long enough to tap into the specific wistfulness of their listeners—some having come of age during the Stones' arc into superstardom. The 1972 *Melody Maker* review of "Tumbling Dice" articulated the significance of the song's release, via the band itself, noting, "It is impossible to see their names on the label and not undergo inner convulsions in which joy, mirth, tears, nostalgia and deep emotion are inevitably interwoven."

And this is more or less my reaction to the whole record. But "Tumbling Dice" is a particularly bruised and aching anthem. If it's not the quintessential Stones song, it is at least the quintessential *Exile* song. It presents itself as a swaggering mid- or up-tempo rock & roll number, but seems satisfied to shuffle out with the setting sun, with one of the most mournful codas this side of "Layla." The effect is intensely melancholy, Jagger fading off as if with his tail between his legs, lonely despite all his "I don't need no jewels in my crown" bluster. His words say one thing, but his performance seems to cry, *I'm taking my toys and going home.*

The lyrics provide yet another twist on the "ramblin', gamblin' man" song of American popular music. "I don't really know what people like about it," Jagger has said of the song. "I don't think it's our best stuff. I don't think it has good lyrics. But people seem to really like it, so good for them." Well, again, maybe the lyrics are nothing special, but it barely matters because the performance of the song as a whole is so arresting. Jagger's underestimation of the song for the lyrics is missing the forest for the trees. "You're no good, heart-breaker, you're a liar and you're a cheat" doesn't seem like much if taken out of context (or worse, in the wrong hands musically) but in Aretha Franklin's "I Never Loved a Man the Way that I Love You," it might be one of pop music's all time greatest opening lines. Soul lyrics can often be trite when simply read on the page, but in the right arrangement, with a great band and a top singer, the lyrics barely matter. And Jagger is a top singer at the top of his game on "Tumbling Dice."

I talked to Graham Parker about his recollection as a fan upon the release of the single. He told me:

They had a competition, I reckon in the *NME*, to see who could get the lyrics for "Tumblin' Dice" right. Someone did, but some joker wrote something like: "Fibby flibby flabby, yibby yibby yabby, make me burna camel right down-wow wow wown," which I thought was a great crack, too . . .

I do recall there was a bit of controversy in the press at the time (at least in either the *Melody Maker* or the *NME*) about the vocal mix. There was an interview with Jagger in one of those rags and they commented on it. He said, rather vaguely, something like: "I don't think they put out the right mixes," which I thought was hilarious!

Soon after the release of the record, Jagger did indeed tell the *Melody Maker*, "I think they used the wrong mix on that one. I'm sure they did." Robert Greenfield of *Rolling Stone* was present during some of the final mixing sessions for *Exile*. He describes Jagger listening back to the mixes of "Tumbling Dice" and saying "They're both good, you know, Jimmy (Miller)." Greenfield notes that it more or less came down to a toss-up when Jimmy Miller noted one mix sounded slightly more "commercial."

The lyrics also barely matter because, as Parker noted, most of us have our own versions in our heads. Mine persist even years after being corrected and seeing the written lyrics, and I enjoy them more than the real ones. Jagger never liked printing lyrics. This is a lesson taken to heart by REM on their early records: write some enigmatic phrases that sound good musically, mix them low, and let the listeners bring their own perceptions to the table. It's a nice formula that produces great results in the right hands.

"We'll get the track when it's hot and write the verses later," Richards explained to *Mojo*. "I'm like, 'The beat goes like this, this is the chorus, um-um-um Tumbling Dice,' and Mick would take it away, because he knows what I'm talking about."

But though the lyrics might have been cobbled together, they put forth that same *Exile* weariness, colored even more by Jagger's warmly worn voice. Even as he offers the variation on typical macho bluesman clichés like "women think I'm tasty," he follows it right up with the next lines: "they're always trying to waste me / make me burn the candlelight down," deflating his own macho arrogance. And we do get some lines key to the record, including "say now baby, I'm the rank outsider / you can be my partner in crime," fitting in with the theme of the exile and artist-outsider. We also see one of the first signs on the record that in songs ostensibly about women, Jagger's lyrics might actually be inspired by his relationship with Richards, who has been his "partner in crime" for longer than any woman in his life. ("He knows what I'm talking about," said Keith; a significant line.) It is just a small example, one that seems more apparent on such songs as "Let It Loose" and "Shine a Light."

Arguably the most effortless sounding, archetypal Rolling Stones song, "Tumbling Dice" was actually one of the hardest to capture. The song sounds so loose that countless other acts tried to capture the same loosey-goose feel, including Rod Stewart, who reportedly brought a tape into the studio for his *Footloose and Fancy Free* LP to try and steer his band in the right direction on "Hot Legs." Andy Johns recalls that the Stones "had a hundred reels of tape on the basic track. That was a good song, but it was really like pulling teeth. It just went on and on."

To hear a few samples of what Johns described as the worst-sounding band clicking into the best in the world, all one has to do is track down bootleg copies of the song's previous incarnations, including "Good Time Women," a throw-away right down to its working title. There have been a few recorded incarnations of the song in circulation. I am aware of a more straightforward blues version, and this "Good Time Women," which is in the "Jiving Sister Fanny" (from *Metamorphosis*) vein, though not as compelling. Certainly, it doesn't much resemble "Tumbling Dice." There is another version closer to the final one, with most of the words and musical characteristics, though it's even slower, lazier, and sloppier. Some collectors note versions stretching back as early as the spring of 1970, during the sessions for *Sticky Fingers*. Bill Wyman's book notes that "Tumbling Dice" was among seven tracks that had been started before the Stones got to France, either at Stargroves or Olympic Studios in London. But Keith recalls writing the riff at Villefranche: "I remember writing the riff upstairs in the very elegant front room, and we took it downstairs the same evening and we cut it. A lot of time when ideas come that quick, we don't put down lyrics, we do what we call vowel movement. You just bellow over the top of it, to get the right sounds for the track." But Johns claims that the particular track went on "for a couple of weeks at least, just the basic track."

The guitars chug along with that trademark Richards ease, right in the pocket. Jagger's battered voice is impossibly low in the mix, drawling, singing like a gospel singer, calling and responding to the background singers, Clydie King and Venetta Field, who make their appearance prominently in third bar of the song and remain featured throughout. Keith's and Mick Taylor's guitars are also far up in the mix, and behind it all, like everywhere on the record, is Nicky Hopkins' piano, sounding like a slightly out-of-tune upright, teasing boogie-woogie triplets everywhere. His high-octave figures during the coda are particularly affecting. Bobby Keys and Jim Price are here as well, of course. Jagger stakes his claim, yet again, as one of the best white vamp singers around. As Lenny Kaye noted in his mixed *Rolling Stone* review at the time, "As the guitar figure slowly falls into Charlie's inevitable smack, the song builds to the kind of majesty the Stones at their best have always provided. Nothing is out of place here. Keith's simple guitar figure providing the nicest of bridges, the chorus touching the upper levels of heaven and spurring on Jagger, set up by an arrangement that is both unique and imaginative."

Jimmy Miller shares drum duty, most likely in the coda, where someone keeps the African-style tom-toms steady. As Joe "No Beatles, No Stones" Strummer pointed out, "it surges forward, but it's not a straightforward tempo. It's halfway between a slow and a straightforward rocker. It has a mystical beat." The singers King and Field might be joined by Merry Clayton, known to Stones fans for her chilling performance on "Gimme Shelter." But in one of many cases of failing to providing the proper credits on the record, the Stones failed to identify the singers correctly, even on the subsequent Virgin CD reissue of *Exile on Main St.*, listing the singers as "clydie king, vanetta, plus friend." Bill Wyman's book *Rolling with the Stones* sets out to correct the oversight, but does not list Clayton. Mick Taylor is on the bass, as Wyman notes blankly: "On 3 August we worked on 'Good Time Woman' and when I arrived the following day I found Mick Taylor playing bass. I hung around until 3am, then left."

Under the black, white, and gray cover of *Exile on Main St.*, we can hear the shades of gray, the in-betweens, the pain, the ennui, and the fallout. "*Exile* is about casualties, and partying in the face of them. The party is obvious. The casualties are inevitable," wrote Lester Bangs. "It is the search for alternatives, something to *do* (something worthwhile even) that unites us with the Stones, continuously." And this is how the band manages to click with listeners on *Exile on Main St.* and other records, even as they distance themselves in other ways. They are exiles in that respect as well, moving farther away from their public—a gulf which, in subsequent years, became unbridgeable and led to increasingly banal music with out-of-touch lyrics, in the opinions of many fans. But on *Exile*, maybe *especially* on *Exile*, the Stones still offered "a strange kind of humility and love emerging from a dazed frenzy."

Though not in the context of "Tumbling Dice" specifically, in *The True Adventures of the Rolling Stones*, Stanley Booth also quotes Willie McTell's "The Dying Crapshooter's Blues."

Folks, don't be standin' around little Jesse cryin'
He wants everybody to do the Charleston whilst he's dyin'

This "partying in the face of it" can be heard on "Tumbling Dice." It is funky and slinky, sexy, though not as convincing at the "partying" aspect as "Rip This Joint" or "All Down the Line." What we hear on "Tumbling Dice" is mostly the other half: "in the face of it." A drained and vulnerable Jagger spins a protagonist moving on, though he sounds like his years are starting to weigh on him, even as his words try to tell us "oh my, my, my, I'm the lone crap shooter / playing the field every night." Even here he is the "lone" gambler, perhaps under the McTell influence. And where Richards, Jagger's real "partner in crime," might have provided a beefy guitar riff and a torrid tempo as a counterpoint, the music is instead loose and easy going, relaxed, perhaps signaling the end of the party; uptempo, but certainly not offering the self-assured maelstrom of "Rip This Joint" or the raging musical counterpoint Keith provides to Jagger's expressed numbness in "Rocks Off."

"Tumbling Dice" was the perfect song for 1972; moving forward reluctantly, alone even, the party continuing even as the "casualties" fell. But *Exile on Main St.* would not finish before sounding off dire laments on such songs as "Soul Survivor," "Let It Loose," and "Shine a Light."

"I really loved 'Tumbling Dice,'" said Keith. "Beautifully played by everybody. When everybody hits it, that's those moments of triumph."

Sweet Virginia

"Mick and Keith liked a few of my songs and we gotta lotta kicks outta just sitting around playing together. All I did was sing and pick with the Stones."—Gram Parsons, *Melody Maker*, May 12, 1973

"Gram (Parsons) is on *Exile* in spirit, but playing? No, not that I can remember."—Keith Richards, *Mojo* magazine, January 2002

It has often been said that the four sides of *Exile on Main St.* represent four distinct records. "Tumbling Dice" closes side one of the original two-record vinyl set, ambling off in a melancholic reverie. How do the Stones answer this as side two begins?

"Sweet Virginia" is wholly different in feel, a simple acoustic campfire sing-along; a country ditty that combines the lyrical influence of honky-tonk man Faron Young, the reedy harmonica of Roy Acuff, and a brassy rock & roll sax; the perfect beginning to an acoustic-based, country and folk-tinged side of songs. The Stones were, for the moment, easy in the niche they carved out of country-rock, which was pervading the airwaves and the album collections of rock & roll fans.

If we want to mark 1968 as a beginning for what seemed to be the general return-to-roots movement in mainstream rock & roll, with albums like *Music From Big Pink* and *Beggars Banquet* as standing examples, then *Exile on Main St.* was recorded during the full bloom of the trend, and the Stones were at the vanguard. Since the establishment of the band, the Stones had been aficionados of not just blues, but also of country, rock, and soul. All of these elements were evident in even the earliest Stones recordings. Keith noted, "The first time I got on stage and played was with this C&W band."

But it took them until the late 60s to try more straight-up country songs—mainly due to a lack of confidence on Jagger's part. "I love country music, but I find it very hard to take it seriously," Jagger has said. "I also think a lot of country music is sung with the tongue in cheek, so I do it tongue in cheek. The harmonic thing is very different from the blues. It doesn't bend notes in the same way, so I suppose it's very English, really. Even though it's been very Americanized, it feels very close to me, to my roots, so to speak."

You wish Jagger would just keep his mask off. He can sing such music convincingly: witness "Wild Horses" and "Sweet Virginia." Still, Mick can't resist acknowledging the well-worn insult of country as "shit-kicking" music in the latter song. He sings these, and other ostensibly country songs, more or less as himself, with no fake accents aside from his usual, well-honed American twang. And the effect actually takes the songs away from the sound of English guys imitating country music; it becomes something else altogether: the Rolling Stones. We don't necessarily think "country music" when we hear "Wild Horses." We do when we hear "Far Away Eyes," as fun as it might be. And we don't let the awareness that the band is under the influence of country effect our reaction to the song.

The influences are evident on "Sweet Virginia." It starts out with the wheezing part Mick plays on the harmonica, bringing back that Jimmie Rodgers vibe and reminding fans of classic C&W of the country fiddle parts heard on numbers by such country legends as Roy Acuff and Faron Young. Those two artists, in particular, come to mind when I hear this song. As with a classic Acuff song like "Wreck on the Highway," or any number of Louvin Brothers tunes, "Sweet Virginia" is more of a country-gospel than a Jimmie Rodgers kind of country-blues in inspiration and form, especially in the chorus refrain device. But while the Louvins were often overtly religious in content, the Stones take the sacred inspiration and secularize the lyric. Meanwhile, they adapt the country-gospel framework and hang on it other influences.

"Sweet Virginia" apparently started at Jagger's Stargroves mansion in the summer of 1970, while songs were still being recorded for *Sticky Fingers*, and was finished at the final Los Angeles sessions. But Dominique Tarlé remembers them recording "Sweet Virginia" and "Sweet Black Angel" in the basement kitchen of Nellcôte, a notion more agreeable to the myth of *Exile*. Nevertheless, it was a similar vibe at Stargroves, what with the big old house and the mobile unit.

"The house that we used, Stargroves, was ideally suited because it was a big mansion and a kind of grand hall with a gallery around with bedroom doors and a staircase," Andy Johns explained. "Big fireplace, big bay window—you could put Charlie in the bay window. And, off the main hall there were other rooms you could put people in. We did stuff like 'Bitch' there, and you can hear on 'Moonlight Mile' when Mick is singing with the acoustic, it sounds very live, because it was! 4 or 5 in the morning, with the sun about to come up, getting takes. It was all very heady stuff for a young chap!"

The band did not tour (aside from a few dates in England) between the two albums, further bonding the records in the minds of many, including Keith Richards.

"Some songs—'Sweet Virginia'—were held over from *Sticky Fingers*," he explained. "It was the same line-up and I've always felt those two albums kind of fold into each other . . . there was not much time between them and I think it was all flying out of the same kind of energy."

"Sweet Virginia" does feel like one of the most off-the-cuff tracks on *Exile on Main St.* Certainly, the same murky atmosphere is present. As Keith starts his opening strum on the acoustic (left side of your stereo), someone bumps a microphone or the guitar within the first bar, only adding to the charm and spontaneous feel. This is a rough-shod production, even looser in feel than "Tumbling Dice." The mastering of the vinyl copy sounds like it might have been botched, because for all my years of listening it sounded as if a compressor or dynamic limiter kicked in too forcefully and quickly on the first chorus' "so come on, come on down . . . " Even listening to it on CD, I still hear the dramatic volume downshift, like those skips and snaps from your original vinyl records that persist as phantoms in your head long after you have replaced the worn-out versions.

The arrangement builds perfectly, as if musicians are just wandering into the room, picking up an instrument, and joining in, clapping hands. The beginning echoes "Country Honk" from *Let it Bleed*. Mick Taylor is off to the right, doubling Jagger's harmonica melody with a fast-picked fake "mandolin" part, and picking seventh chords and major-scale and country-blues runs throughout. Charlie keeps it simple, with just a big double-headed kick (hollow sounding) and a snare drum, no cymbals or tom-toms. Bill Wyman is credited with bass, but it sounds suspiciously like a stand-up bass, which would most likely have been overdubbed by Bill Plummer in Los Angeles. If not, Wyman either plays a bass fiddle himself, or does a convincing job making his electric bass sound like one. And in fact, in outtake versions, the bass does sound like an electric, perhaps a hollow body, mimicking an upright. On Wyman's final take, he simplifies his part, and on both versions, he swings.

Ian Stewart joins in on the second verse with a rollicking boogie-woogie part straight out of the songbook of his primary influence, Albert Ammons. Impossibly behind the beat, Stewart effortlessly reels off inspired riffs, the sort for which he was best known. It is counterintuitive that Stu is on here to begin with; as the most "country" of the songs, "Sweet Virginia" would seem at first glance to beg for the Floyd Cramer style of "slipnote" country frills that Nicky Hopkins adopted. Yet it's just that tension of the straight-up country elements coupled with the boogie-woogie texture that makes the song so compelling. The rhythmic movement of Stu's piano part propels the song.

Bobby Keys adds a few sax licks off in the background, waiting his turn to solo, wrenching the song from the Chicago boogie-woogie pull of Stu down toward the New Orleans or East Texas juke-joint R&B of someone like Professor Longhair or King Curtis.

Meanwhile, Jagger does his best to bring us to a country church somewhere in the deep South, in a performance that begins with him sounding like he's picking up where he left off on "Tumbling Dice," or even a bit wearier, and ends in an incredibly spirited call-and-response with the backing vocalists. One of the best moments seems to be an inspired bit of spontaneity as one of the female backing singers (uncredited, of course) suddenly takes the lead part, while Jagger recedes and willfully joins the chorus (heard at around 3:46). His vocal part sounds almost mush-mouthed, as if he is out of breath from his harmonica part, a bit drunk, his voice cracking on the words "winter" and "friend."

The title likely comes—perhaps unconsciously—from Mamie Smith's 1926 "Sweet Virginia Blues," but Jagger's lyric appears to be inspired by a variety of sources. In some lines, it sounds like he's expressing concern for a friend. The first verse of "Sweet Virginia" is more of a sympathy bit, with sentiments that would be heard again on such songs as "Winter" and "Coming Down Again" on the next album, *Goats Head Soup*. "Sweet Virginia" begins:

> *Wading through the waste, stormy winter*
> *And there's not a friend to help you through*
> *Trying to stop the waves behind your eyeballs*
> *Drop your reds, drop your greens and blues*

The next verse gets really interesting. Jagger seems to take direct inspiration from honky-tonk legend Faron Young's "Wine Me Up," which has the verse:

I'd like to thank the men that raise the grapes way out in California
And I'm hoping this will be their biggest year
'Cause scarlet water's all that's left to keep me hanging on

From Shreveport, Louisiana, Faron Young had been a Grand Ole Opry star since the 1950s. But "Wine Me Up" was a comeback hit single on the country charts in 1969, and the Stones might have heard it while they were recording at Muscle Shoals in Alabama.

Mick sings:

> *Thank you for your wine, California*
> *Thank you for your sweet and bitter fruits*
> *Yes, I've got the desert in my toenail*
> *And I hid the speed inside my shoe*

Still mired in the fallout of Altamont, California would indeed have been a bitter taste in Jagger's mouth.

The desert he sings of might be an allusion to the desert-like Altamont—located just outside Livermore, California, which was known for its wine-producing vineyards until the prominence of Napa Valley overshadowed it. And most accounts of the Stones' show at Altamont feature people sharing big jugs of wine. The allusion to Altamont resonates throughout the song, with Jagger continuing the *Exile on Main St.* theme of moving on, leaving those bad tastes from the 60s behind. The fistfuls of color-coded pills he sings about also reference the lifestyle in the Stones' orbit circa 1971. The lyric is one of willful alienation, the continued outsider perspective; drugs taking you out of one shared reality for another, trying to "help you through." Jagger yearns for salvation of some kind here, whether the "Virginia" he beckons is a woman, a friend, a place, a state of mind, or all of the above.

That state of mind was almost certainly inspired in part by the ever-present Gram Parsons, a man closely and forever identified with the Joshua Tree area of the Mojave desert, though he himself may or may not be on the track. Mick Taylor claimed, "I know it's rumored that he sang backing vocals on 'Sweet Virginia' but that is me singing, not him." And I asked Al Perkins, a friend and collaborator of Gram's, and the pedal steel guitarist who plays on "Torn and Frayed," if he recalls Gram being anywhere on *Exile* and he gave me an unequivocal "no," mentioning that Gram was not even at the session in Los Angeles during which Perkins recorded his part. Of course, Perkins was not present in France, so who knows for sure? Bill Wyman lists Parsons as "additional personnel" in his *Rolling with the Stones*. All of this just adds to the "mystery" of *Exile on Main St.*

Since I was a child, my favorite records have always had moments that make me wish I had been part of the action when the recording went down, like I missed out on the party. This is one reason I wanted to become a musician and a member in a band. "Sweet Virginia" might be the best example of this sort of song. The lyrics knowingly nudge the listener, drawing you in with the sense that you're in on the sentiment, if not the actual party; in lieu of a "friend to help you through," you've got your sympathetic friends in the Stones to do so. Mick might not be the same sort of "bridge over troubled water" that Simon and Garfunkel offered, but he's there to hear you and perhaps provide some medicinal support with "reds . . . greens and blues." The sing-along makes you want to be a part of the group. And the three-chord structure of the song made it an easy one to play at parties from junior high school to college and beyond. If it's possible to pinpoint specific moments in my path toward becoming a rock & roller, hearing "Sweet Virginia" is chief among them. I would play this song over and over again when I first got *Exile on Main*

St. It's a song that begs for continued spins, and the famous DJ Wolfman Jack went out on a limb and heavily promoted this non-single album track on his radio show on KDAY in Los Angeles.

Torn and Frayed

An autumnal, melancholy song, "Torn and Frayed" has, like "Sweet Virginia," been called "country," though it seems this is just for lack of a better term. But with its strong rock & roll backbeat, the song is closer to the "southern rock" of the Allman Brothers ("Sweet Melissa") than the country rock of Parsons, the Eagles, and others. Bill Wyman is clearly not playing bass, as only a guitar player—scratch that, only a *lead* guitar player—would play a part as busy as the bass maelstrom Mick Taylor works up by the second verse of the song.

Again, we have a predominantly three-chord structure that has as many roots in gospel as it does in country, with more similarities to the southern soul of Memphis and Muscle Shoals than to Nashville country. The main difference lies in Mick's vocals, slurring notes like an R&B singer rather than a straight country singer. Such singers as Ray Charles, on one side, and George Jones, on the other, could also blur the distinctions between soul and country. Country, after all, has been defined as white man's blues. Jagger is another who successfully melds the two approaches.

Though driven by Keith's acoustic guitar, there is a deep layered sound that builds from this gentle strumming to a provocative mix of steel guitar, wheezing organ, piano, country-clean electric Telecaster guitar picking, and densely-packed lead and backing vocals. The most spirit-lifting of all these sounds is the chiming combination of Jim Price's organ and Al Perkins' pedal steel.

Trumpet player Price was apparently just listening to the band as they did the basic tracks and started to fool around on the organ, not realizing he was being heard and recorded. "All the different instruments were set up in different rooms," he recalls in Appleford's book. "I went into that room, picked up the headphones and started listening and just started playing the organ. It was just for fun. They did a bunch of takes on it, and I never knew that they had used it until I saw it on the record."

Perkins was brought in at the Los Angeles sessions at Sunset Sound with Mick, Keith, and Anita Pallenberg. He told me he had just gotten a new pedal steel guitar, "from an eight-string Fender to an eleven-string ZB Custom of Tom Brumley's, with loads of levers and pedals." I asked him if he did many takes, perhaps still getting used to the quirks of the new instrument. "Not very many," he replied. "But Mick sang and did his stage action each time to give me some live feeling." Noting that the sound of the steel blends so well with the organ, I asked him if recalled playing off of Price's part in particular. "Frankly, I think it was presented a bit sparse, if memory serves me correctly, but I also think it would have been one of the last overdubs."

The character of the song's protagonist seems to blend elements of Keith and Gram Parsons, though it could be any one of a number of characters familiar to Jagger, including many of the parasitic hangers-on in Keith's orbit: "Just a dead beat right off the street / bound to follow you down." It is a picture of a ragged, vagabond guitar player named Joe, who we follow from "smelly bordellos" though "dressing rooms filled with parasites." As Robert Greenfield, who followed the Stones on their 1971 tour of England, noted in *Rolling Stone*, the Stones were no strangers to less-than-luxurious dressing rooms, even as late as that very tour, as the world's most successful rock & roll band: "In Glasgow, one of life's cheap plastic dramas. Green's Playhouse. Paint peeling off the walls. Six inches of soot in the air vents. Bare bulbs backstage and fluorescent tubes for house lights. The third balcony is closed 'to keep the raytes doon.'"

Jagger keeps spinning the yarn of ragged glory with an ease of language, words rolling off his tongue like the lyrics of Chuck Berry and Hank Williams—the sound and rhythm as important as the words themselves:

> *Joe's got a cough, sounds kind of rough*
> *Yeah, and the codeine to fix it*
> *Doctor prescribes, drugstore supplies*
> *Who's going to help him to kick it?*

I used to hear that last verse line as "who's gonna help in the kitchen?" which to me was symbolic of the whole myth of *Exile on Main St.* as a bunch of friends living communally in the torn and frayed Nellcôte mansion, recording and fixing meals all in the same kitchen, a myth that holds a certain degree of truth, as it turns out. Who needs lyric sheets?

Jagger is sympathetic to the character of Joe, who probably reflects Gram Parsons more than Keith Richards. Stanley Booth details a few jaunts the Stones' entourage took out to seedy Los Angeles-area clubs to see Gram and the Flying Burrito Brothers play, with Gram stealing their hearts away. Al Perkins points out that, while other groups in the late 1960s might have been consciously going back to the roots of rock & roll for newfound inspiration and rejuvenation, guys like Parsons were really just playing what was most natural for them. "I also believe people like Chris Hillman, Gram, and even Ricky Nelson were at last able to perform, their way, a style of music they'd grown up with," he observed.

Gram, a trust-fund kid, was as restless a searcher and wanderer as Keith, one also interested in the mythology/reality dichotomy of America. Stanley Booth, a Georgian who felt an attachment to Parsons, recalls a 1969 conversation he had with Gram high in a hotel tower on Sunset Boulevard while waiting for the Stones to commence their American tour:

> "Look at it, man," he said, as if he had read my thoughts. "They call it America, and they call it civilization, and they call it television, and they believe in it and salute it and sing songs to it and eat and sleep and die still believing in it, and—and—I don't know," he said, taking another drag, "then sometimes the Mets come along and win the World Series."

Sweet Black Angel

Three little Injuns out in a canoe,
One tumbled overboard and then there were two.
Two little Injuns foolin' with a gun,
One shot t'other and then there was one;

One little Injuns livin' all alone,
He got married and then there were none
　　　　　　Ten Little Indians—Septimus Winner, 1868

Seven little nigger boys chopping up sticks;
One chopped himself in half, and then there were six.

Six little nigger boys playing with a hive;
A bumble-bee stung one, and then there were five.

Five little nigger boys going in for law;
One got in chancery, and then there were four.

Ten Little Niggers—Frank Green, 1869

Mick Jagger is certain to have been familiar with some variation of "Ten Little Niggers," Frank Green's English music-hall adaptation of Septimus Winner's "Ten Little Indians." Winner wrote many "comic" songs for the American minstrel circuit and was once jailed for treason for penning "Give Us Back Our Old Commander," a song critical of President Abraham Lincoln. On "Sweet Black Angel," Jagger, in a sort of blackface of his own, takes his inspiration from the travails of Angela Davis, an African-American UCLA professor who some parties also accused of treason—a piece of symmetry that was likely coincidental.

In 1969, Governor Ronald Reagan had exerted pressure on the California Regents Board to dismiss Davis from her teaching post, due to her Marxist views and membership in the communist party. After a judge ruled that this was not legal grounds for such a dismissal, "the Regents again voted to remove her, this time for 'inflammatory' speeches she had made that were critical of University policy," according to a *New York Times* report at the time.

In August of 1970, Davis was arrested and went to trial for conspiracy in the murder of four people, including a judge, at a Marin County courthouse. The crimes occurred during a botched escape attempt by self-proclaimed revolutionary prisoners the "Soledad Brothers." (Davis had championed the cause of one of them.) The weapons used during the crimes were allegedly registered in her name. She evaded capture until October of that same year and was finally arrested in a motel in New York. Her trial began in the summer of 1972; Davis was ultimately acquitted of all charges by an all-white jury. In the meantime, hers became a *cause célèbre*. Her image became iconic: a strikingly beautiful woman with a large natural afro, saluting black power with her fist held high. In a June 1971 *New York Times* article, Sol Stern wrote:

> At the hearings, she walks in briskly, trailing her matrons behind her, and turns, very tall and regal, to give spectators the clenched-fist salute. She wears bright mini-dresses, and in the soft lights reflecting off the hand-rubbed walnut furniture (made by state prison inmates), she glows with a tawny, imperious beauty. At her table she sits upright and attentive, conferring animatedly with her lawyers, her dignity hardly bruised by six months in jail.

Dignity is an essential undercurrent of *Exile*. There is a nagging suggestion underpinning the album's lyrics that perhaps the guys in the Stones are getting too old for all the ridiculousness that surrounds them. But equally as important, there is another prong suggesting that their generation got a lot of things right, and Davis was symbolic of the legitimate struggle against the status quo and the old guard. And they likely identified with her as another lightning rod for controversy, as someone who had experienced steady pressure from the authorities. "I think we put the picture of her up on the wall after the song, but Angela was all over that album," recalled Keith Richards. "She was on T-shirts. She was real big at the time." Mick Taylor noted, "I think Mick (Jagger) wrote the song first, then thought it could be about Angela Davis afterwards. Everybody was fairly politicized because in 1972 the Vietnam War was coming to an end. We didn't have a TV at Nellcôte so we never saw the news, we used to read the English papers."

The song began its recorded life in 1970 as the instrumental "Bent Green Needles," up at Stargroves. Jagger started adding the topical lyrics as the tenor of the times crept in to Nellcôte. The intent is one of clear support for Davis, referenced specifically in lines like "she's a sweet back angel, not a gun-toting teacher." Mick is daringly ironic in his lyric, adopting a voice in full minstrel mode, unflinchingly quoting the highly charged word "nigger" from the politically incorrect early Frank Green song, which he had probably heard at least in the nursery rhyme version (which was also taken as a title for an Agatha Christie novel and subsequent play and film adaptations). In placing the trial of Davis within that context, via a Caribbean-flavored folk song, Jagger celebrates Davis as a full-fledged folk hero and legend.

> *Ten little niggers sitting on the wall*
> *Her brothers been falling, falling one by one*
> *For a judge's murder in a judge's court*
> *Now the judge he going to judge her for all that*
>   *he's worth*

Jagger cleverly twists the old racist song into a metaphor for the trial and the militant arm of the civil rights movement of the late 1960s, rightly positing it as a life-and-death struggle. In less capable hands, the lyric might come off as minstrelsy of the worst sort: mockery for the sake of entertainment. But Mick co-opts the lines in support of a cause that neither Winner nor Green would likely have anticipated. In doing so, he aims to diffuse the sting of that original bigotry, and turns it in on itself, making it look ridiculous. Moreover, the alliterative words sound simply great within the rhythm and melody of the song. And Mick never breaks out of that character/narrator, singing lines like, "not a Red-loving school marm," which smoothly fit a current subject into the framework and language of an old Jamaican sort of folk song. The Stones bring that same air of authenticity and timelessness to the song that the Band and Dylan captured back in the late 1960s.

The narrative voice operates on multiple levels. Some critics might have considered the Rolling Stones' history of copping African-American music as a kind of cultural exploitation, similar to that practiced by all-white minstrel companies. But Jagger is in on the joke; the Stones themselves could be misconstrued as an updated minstrel show. While arguments have been made that—buried under the exploitation and mockery—minstrelsy had the positive byproduct of allowing give-and-take between European-American and African-American musical forms, especially as African-Americans themselves started to integrate the minstrel troupes, Jagger would certainly have been sensitive to such matters. He does not let any self-consciousness impede on "Sweet Black Angel," though; rather, he displays a solid confidence in his own motives.

Musically, the transition of "Torn and Frayed" into "Sweet Black Angel" is one of *Exile*'s most pleasing. The music and lyrics approximate Jamaican *mento*: a mix of mostly West African and Spanish influences that served as a precursor to ska and reggae. Keith starts it with a complicated rhythm on rich acoustic guitar and is joined by Jimmy Miller playing percussion on a guiro (the ridged instrument you drag a stick across) and woodblock. The marimbas are another distinguishing characteristic, played by Richard "Didymus" Washington, credited as "Amyl Nitrate." A New Orleans musician, he had been brought into the Los Angeles sessions by Dr. John. Bill Wyman fits a slippery bass part into the acoustic rhythm.

Jagger plays a compelling harmonica part and sings a gorgeous melody in a faux-Jamaican accent, the sort of affectation he would employ throughout the 1970s and 80s, with mixed results. He is clearly performing here, in character. Intertwined are compelling harmonies from Keith and Mick himself. As with "Sweet Virginia," there is a campfire feel to the song. "That was done all of them in a room in a circle at the same time, because there was this one room away from the main hall that had no furniture in it, with a wooden floor, quite high ceilings and plaster walls," said Andy Johns, recalling the set-up at Stargroves (though Dominque Tarlé recalls it being recorded in the same kitchen at Nellcôte as "Sweet Virginia"). "We wanted to get the sound of the room." "Sweet Black Angel" made for an inspired and infectious choice as the b-side of the "Tumbling Dice" single.

Loving Cup

We get another of *Exile*'s most satisfying segues as "Sweet Black Angel" fades and up comes one of Nicky Hopkins' shining moments, introducing "Loving Cup" with a booming gospel piano part. He's out there all alone without a net for the first thirteen seconds of the song, a deserved solo moment for this brilliant player. The vocals chime in—Mick's melody and Keith's tight, reedy harmony—a defining texture.

"Loving Cup" sounds like a microcosmic representation of what I, in my idealized version of the *Exile* myth, would picture as the perfect day down at Villefranche-Sur-Mer, the sunny piano part brimming with the optimism that can only come on a summer morning. Jagger joins in as if inspired by it, beaming with a happy-go-lucky, self-deprecating lyric that reflects the ramshackle vibe down in Villefranche:

> *I'm the man on the mountain, come on up*
> *I'm the plowman in the valley with a face full of mud*
> *Yes I'm fumbling and I know my car don't start*
> *Yes I'm stumbling and I know I play a bad guitar*

Though it's hard to picture Mick with mud on his face, his body aching with tired satisfaction after a day's honest labor, here he is as a humble, salt-of-the-earth guy with simple needs, with all made well again by his woman:

> *Give me a little drink from your loving cup*
> *Just one drink and I'll fall down drunk*

These all sound like images from the surroundings in which the Stones found themselves. We see them in pictures from those days walking "the hillside in the sweet summer sun." We have the sort of uplift that comes from the sensuousness the words express, visceral and earthy images like "face full of mud," "run and jump and fish," and "nitty, gritty, and my shirt's all torn." We have Jagger's narrator kissing "in front of the fire." We can hear the Stones embracing these elements of an agrarian ideal.

The morning of the lyric extends into afternoon, as the band joins in bit by bit; shakers and acoustic guitar riffing at about 0:18, Keith and Nicky interweaving, playing off of each other. The rest of the band—Bill Wyman on bass (agile, as always) and what sounds like Keith on electric guitar—tumble in, driven by Charlie Watts' authoritative drum fill at about fifty seconds into the song. The activity of the day begins picking up: "well I can run and jump and fish but I won't fight / you if you want to push and pull with me all night," a particularly satisfying poetic line break.

This all leads to one of my favorite middle-eight bridges in pop music, the group just about dropping out, screeching to a halt with bits of stray vocal improvisations carrying over as the arrangement strips down to just the percussive elements holding it all together. The section opens up for the regal horns of Jim Price and Bobby Keys ("I feel so humble with you tonight just sitting in front of the fire"). It is an intricate, lush horn arrangement, a cross between a New Orleans funeral and a sublime martial ceremony; a soaring, uplifting, almost holy moment, like a fanfare for a king (albeit, one in exile). Then the band picks up again, Hopkins begins to hammer the keyboard as Charlie counts time with increasing volume, leading to the fills that spill onto one of the record's most memorable couplets, voiced forcefully by Jagger and Richards in harmony: "well I am nitty, gritty, and my shirt's all torn / but I would love to spill the beans with you 'til dawn."

These lines, as with the lyrics of "Happy," suggest a clever update to Tin Pan Alley-era turns of phrase, but the whole song breezes along with an ease of language that betrays such cleverness, with Mick singing an uncomplicated lyric in natural vernacular. Listen carefully and you can hear Jagger singing the "spill the beans" line as an overlap to a previous line on one of his unison parts. Earlier versions of the song (they ran through it at Muscle Shoals in 1969 and a facsimile of it was played at the Hyde Park concert as "Give Me a Drink") have the bridge occurring twice; one time Mick sings "dirt, gritty . . ." and "I would love to push and pull with you 'til dawn," which is probably what remains under there on the final mix. But previous recordings sound plodding and overly loose. The final version, as with "Tumbling Dice" and so many others, rides one of those perfect Stones grooves.

The horns return for the coda ending section, with a far more raucous chart than the bridge, adding a trombone in the low register. Nicky plays high-octave triplets, while the backing singers (Gram Parsons again rumored to be among them) do a call-and-response with an improvising Mick. And as I write this, wearing headphones, I experience one of those moments of discovery, finding yet another texture. I could swear I hear a subtle steel drum part, or something that sounds a lot like one, down in the mix, from 3:38 until the end of the song, playing a rhythmic and melodic counterpoint to both the "gimme little drink" chorus and the horn part. Listen for yourself; it's on the left side.

Ultimately, the day cycle of the song empties onto the dawn of the next. While *Exile on Main St.* has the image of a bleak and dark record, there are plenty of moments when the sun is allowed to seep in, with "All Down the Line" and "Happy" also representing the light alongside "Loving Cup." Nick Hornby, discussing pop music in general, wrote in 2004, "there is still a part of me that persists in thinking that rock music, and indeed all art, has an occasional role to play in the increasingly tricky art of making us glad we're alive," which is exactly how I feel about "Loving Cup." My newest convert is my daughter, who has insisted since age three that we listen to the song daily on our drive to her preschool. I gladly oblige. The cycle continues.

Happy

On "Happy," the Human Riff unleashes one of his absolute classics. Keith opens with that sort of tension-filled guitar figure that bops and weaves all around the beat, making the listener wonder how he is finally ever going to make it into the beat itself. He has a way of swinging guitar riffs so severely that they sound like false starts, paying as much mind to the upbeat as the down, small aural tricks that dip and rise dynamically. Taking his sweet time to introduce the song, his open-G-tuned guitar ringing that identifiable four-note lick on one side, doubled by a slide part off on the other, the song is all Keith, almost literally:

> That happened in one grand bash in France for *Exile*. I had the riff. The rest of the Stones were late for one reason or another. It was only Bobby Keys there and Jimmy Miller, who was producing. I said, I've got

this idea; let's put it down for when the guys arrive. I put down some guitar and vocal, Bobby was on baritone sax and Jimmy was on drums. We listened to it, and I said, I can put another guitar there and a bass. By the time the Stones arrived, we'd cut it. I love it when they drip off the end of the fingers. And I was pretty happy about it, which is why it ended up being called "Happy."

We all know it as the signature Keith Richards tune, a declaration of self, his calling card. And if Keith is "Happy," then the band is happy. This is where the rock star myth collects some validity, and it is ground zero for Keith wannabes. Here is the *joie de vivre* that rock & roll is supposed to reflect.

Keith mixes old blues themes in lines like "didn't want to be like Poppa / working for the boss every night and day" with a more nuanced update on Cole Porter:

I get no kick from champagne
Mere alcohol doesn't thrill me at all

Some they may go for cocaine
I'm sure that if, I took even one signature sniff
It would bore me terrifically too
But I get a kick out of you
        —Cole Porter, "I Get a Kick Out of You"

Never got a flash out of cocktails
When I can get some flesh off the bone
      —Keith Richards, "Happy"

I get no kick in a plane
Flying too high with some guy [gal] in the sky
Is my idea of nothing to do
Yet I get a kick out of you

       —Cole Porter

Never got a lift out of Lear jets
When I can fly way back home
I need a love to keep me happy

       —Keith Richards

These thematic parallels may be coincidence, but Keith has always claimed to have his "antenna" up, ready to soak up whatever was in the air. And he has been known to play "I Get a Kick Out of You" later in his career, and bootleg recordings exist of a performance or two of the Porter song.

In addition to a funky, inspired bass part, Richards gives a highly spirited vocal performance on "Happy," supported by prominent backing vocals overdubbed by Jagger, who takes over the ad-lib section at the end, which Keith seems to accede gladly. The song benefits from yet another dazzling mix of many layered components, including dual slide guitar parts, split in stereo.

Jimmy Miller's drums and percussion drive the back-beat. In addition to Bobby Keys' baritone sax, it sounds like he added a tenor horn as well. He had actually just been playing percussion during the basic tracking. Jim Price added trumpet and trombone lines and the arrangement builds to a real horn-heavy drone as the song ends, with interweaving and overlapping horn parts. It all results in a raging hard-rock, maximum R&B attack. Nicky Hopkins hammers away on Wurlitzer electric piano, creating the sort of part that Ian McLagan became known for with the Faces.

As I noted earlier, the sessions for *Exile on Main St.* saw the actors in the drama drifting in and out of Nell-côte at various times throughout the project, and it was often difficult to get the Stones all in one place at one time. But even with this in mind, "Happy" is an extreme case, with one member alone taking hold of the reigns. (Though this was not unheard of: Jagger and Mick Taylor pretty much recorded all of "Moonlight Mile" on *Sticky Fingers* while Keith was away from the studio, or, in his words, "out of it.")

But the way "Happy" went down points to a difference between Keith and Mick in preferred working methods. According to her various accounts, Anita Pallenberg reckons that, not long after the band and their respective families were pulled closer together by their mutual exile from their homeland, a widening gulf started developing between the band members as the time recording *Exile* went on, especially between Mick and Keith. "I never really saw Mick and Keith sitting together and working like they used to in the old days, when they used to rely on each other," she told *Mojo*, further dispelling my closely guarded myth of the sessions. Mick seemed to have the most trouble with the situation, as there was little for him to do when the band was still in the nascent stages of a song, developing from a riff that might have come to Keith in a midnight or morning burst of inspiration. Only as an idea started to gel and it became apparent it would grow into a real song would Jagger start to concentrate on writing proper lyrics, otherwise he was wasting precious resources and inspiration. Mick preferred hatching ideas first with Keith before bringing it to the band at the next stage. Keith, however, liked to catch inspiration as it struck, doing all in his power to capture and exploit whatever magic might happen.

Turd on the Run

"Turd on the Run" takes its place next to "Ventilator Blues" and "Casino Boogie" as one of the churning-urn blues numbers on *Exile*, the songs that seem to have risen out of the torrid basement jam sessions, sweat dripping from the musicians in the middle of the humid

Riviera nights. It would really surprise and impress me if Jagger overdubbed his lead vocal part in Los Angeles later, because I want to believe that he was just down there howling his way through it while the rest of the band ground out the mostly one-chord drone. Jagger offers the kind of hooting, screaming, growling vocal—the essence of raw blues—that punk blues artists like the Cramps and White Stripes worked decades later. Here are the Stones near their most primordial.

This song could never have had any commercial potential, and it might have never even occurred to the Stones that such a raw, decidedly non-pop "song" would even make it onto an album—and if it were any other album, it might not have. But this is *Exile on Main St.*, so the band sounds like they are playing for the sheer exhilaration of it, playing as if the music just needed to come out. Thankfully, it was documented and mixed properly on an official recording, not just tucked away on some murky bootleg. And here is precisely what makes the album so special, and why talk of cutting it down to one record is misguided; where else, aside from bootlegs and in rare live situations, do we get to hear a mainstream, massively successful band stretching out and having fun? And yet, this is no insufferable prog-rock or jam-band experimentation that you will never play again; no, "Turd on the Run" would sit well on a compilation next to Howlin' Wolf, the Clash, or even some faster hardcore punk rock. In fact, the song gets my vote over "Rip This Joint" for the record's most punk rock song. The narrator on "Rip This Joint" sounds like he is just out to have a good time raising hell at the union hall. On "Turd on the Run," Jagger sounds desperate, in pain, driven over the edge, menacingly so. And he sounds like he is going to make someone pay:

> *Begged, promised anything if only you would stay*
> *Well I lost a lot of love on you*
> *YEAH! THAT'S RIGHT!*
>
> *. . . Diamond rings, Vaseline, you gave me disease*
> *Well I lost a lot of love on you!*

Mick blasts away some harp fills right out of the Junior Wells playbook, when he's not yowling like a banshee. Keith is right there with him in a close harmony on choice lines. Stray bits of reverberating vocal, guitar, and harmonica parts drift in and out between the lines. One such spare part that jumped out at me recently is heard at around 0:32 to 0:34: a guitar sound that comes out of nowhere to make a teetering three-note figure repeats, then disappears until the instrumental break, from about 1:01 to 1:35, just droning on with a slight variation on the main riff that Keith is chugging down. Nicky Hopkins bangs away at the piano, boogie-woogie style. Charlie keeps it austerely simple, just swishing away at the snare drum with a steam train beat, allowing the others to rage away on their jam. The ensemble includes Bill Plummer on an overdubbed upright bass, who hides the fact that he overdubbed in LA; he sounds like he might well have been there in the basement, furiously slapping away at the strings, clacking them against the fretboard. But Plummer adds far more than any sort of rockabilly cliché; his part is more like an amphetamine-blues bass. The band sounds possessed by a mutual spirit. As the instrumental parts swirl up into a frenzy, like it's the end of a Baptist church gospel vamp—all they are missing is someone speaking in tongues. But then Mick ups the ante near the end, covering his mouth in rapid taps as he howls a bone-chilling falsetto like a Comanche warrior heading into battle, bringing the song into a haunting fade. You can almost hear the Cramps' Lux Interior presaged here.

Ventilator Blues

Now, deep within the bowels of the album, we find the most malevolent sounding song on *Exile*. "Ventilator Blues" takes a Chess Records template, a hard electric blues worthy of Willie Dixon, Howlin' Wolf, or Muddy Waters. And for one of the few times in his tenure with the Stones, Mick Taylor gets a songwriting credit next to Jagger/Richards. He created the insistent slide guitar lick that runs in an almost nightmarish loop through this claustrophobic song, relentlessly cornering the listener as if in one of the windowless rooms in the moldy basement of Nellcôte—which was, in fact, the inspiration for the immediate lyrical theme. Pointing out some typically small basement windows in a photo in *Exile*, Andy Johns explained, "See these windows here? That was the only air that would come in, so everything would get so hot. The guitars would go out of tune constantly because of the heat. That's why they played 'Ventilator Blues.'"

But the intra-band tension must also have played a part in the shared need to let off a little steam. An unhealthy dose of paranoia set in at Nellcôte, brought on by very real events such as the theft of priceless guitars and the presence of seedy drug dealers ever ready to ply their wares. The drug use within the band itself was only likely to heighten the intensity of the mistrust. The arrangement of this song alone reflects the tension: the band hangs on a single chord for the bulk of the song until, as the lyric suggests, something must give, with an incredible release on the chorus, which nevertheless builds to a subsequent ascending horn-driven climax on the lines "no matter where you are / everybody's gonna need some kind of ventilator." Mick drags on that last line of the chorus well into the next section, as if finally discovering some kind of release for himself.

Mick's vocal, double-tracked in a unison part—a common recording technique, but one that was rarely used on Stones records—bulks up his testosterone-fueled voice as he urgently spews such lines as "woman's cussin' you can hear her scream / sounds like murder in the first degree," and "when your trapped and circled and no second chance / code of livin' is your gun in hand." He pronounces "first" as "foist," "murder" as "moidah," and "learn" as "loin," for that bluesman twang. But once again, the authority of his performance nips in the bud any notion that Jagger is merely indulging in any mimicry. His improvised bits at the end of and between lines are inspired; an assortment of *that's all right*s and *come down and get it*s. And at the end of the song, as the band roils away on the lick to take the song home, Mick spits out a challenge, a provocation as the ending refrain:

> *Whatcha gonna do about? Watcha gonna do?*
> *Gonna fight it?*

On an album of career-defining moments for Nicky Hopkins, his performance on "Ventilator Blues" might be the most awe-inspiring. He is all over the keyboard, raging away like an intense, updated Otis Spann or Pinetop Perkins. After years of listening to this record, and hearing Jagger's vocals and Mick Taylor's slide guitar most prominently on the song, at some point the piano part hit me, grabbed me by the throat, and insisted that I hear it first and foremost on every subsequent listen. The song has never sounded the same to me since. Hopkins plays like a man possessed, slipping impossibly quick figures into the funky, complicated rhythm set by Keith and Charlie. As the arrangement builds, Nicky moves from a comparatively sedate part that sits comfortably in the spaces left by the guitar riff to a jittery, tense hammering style, rolling off triplets up the keyboard with his quick right hand in the higher octaves.

Hopkins adds to an already scary cabin fever tension. He manages this within a rhythm so tricky that Jimmy Miller apparently had to help Watts along as he skips snare beats, also adding to the nervousness of the arrangement. As ardent Stones fan Mike Gent of the bands the Figgs and the Gentlemen explained, "Jimmy Miller got the groove on that together and had to stand over Charlie and clap in time so he could get that fat backbeat down." The horns rise dynamically like a truck sounding its air horn as it barrels uncontrollably down a mountain highway. Bill Wyman plays a grounded bass part worthy of Willie Dixon, and Mick Taylor's slide part just sounds flat out fantastic.

"On 'Ventilator Blues' we got some weird sound of something that had gone wrong—some valve or tube that had gone," Keith said, explaining the happy accidents that sometimes occurred in the less than ideal conditions of the basement. "If something was wrong you just forgot about it. You'd leave it alone and come back tomorrow and hope it had fixed itself. Or give it a good kick." Buried under this entire storm is an acoustic guitar part, which helps to steady the rhythm—holds the fort down, as it were. Such telling details lift songs like "Ventilator Blues" way beyond straight-on hero worship to something more remarkable.

I Just Want to See His Face

In yet another winning transition, "Ventilator Blues" fades as "I Just Want to See His Face" rises from the smoke. Now we really sound like we're in a basement, but one in the deep south, a New Orleans church revival meeting perhaps, or a Creole voodoo chant. The two songs are utterly different in tone, but somehow they fit together. It's as if the same man with his back against the wall on "Ventilator Blues" can somehow be saved from himself on "I Just Want to See His Face": "sometimes you want no trouble, sometimes you feel so down / let this music relax you mind." The narrator doesn't sound convinced that he has found religion, but feels he can be saved by the sight of His mere visage. And you feel like his victim: he's cornered and beaten you to within an inch of your life on "Ventilator Blues," and now he's holding off from finishing the deed, as his unstable mind teeters back and forth between the sacred and the profane, the holy and the murderous. You're okay, though, as long as he keeps singing about Jesus.

This fits the themes of *Exile on Main St.* as a whole: the violence and the chaos are soothed by the music. This song is so necessary to the whole vibe of *Exile*; it would be hard to imagine the record without it. Mick knows what we need better than we do; here is a breather, a meditative moment, a reward for those who listen enough and a gift for those ready to accept. Never mind accepting Jesus, can you accept this little piece of musical salvation into your heart? It articulates my appreciation for—and likely sums up Mick's feeling's about—gospel music; feeling soothed and lifted by the spirit of the songs without necessarily subscribing to the specific religious doctrine behind the lyrics. And there is a long and deep tradition of gospel songs with lyrics reflecting such satisfaction in the mere image or presence of Jesus, as a salve. Take, for example, the Soul Stirrers' song "He's My Friend Until the End":

> *Then one day you'll see God's face*
> *After you'd won this Christian race*
> *He'll be your friend*

The murky basement sound fits into the whole myth of the record. Most accounts of the recording of this haunting song, including Jagger's own, have Mick and Keith sitting around and jamming for a test recording, with Keith at the electric piano. Mick apparently improvised the lines while singing to Keith's hypnotic part. Mick Taylor played bass. The beautiful gospel backing vocals and Bill Plummer's astonishing stand-up bass part were overdubbed later in Los Angeles, after it became apparent that this mesmerizing track could not be rejected.

Yet, contrary to the legend, it might be Bobby Whitlock playing electric piano, appearing on the album uncredited. I talked to Whitlock and mentioned that I saw this mentioned only once—in all the various books, databases, Internet sources, and articles—and offhandedly he confirmed this:

> That's right. Those things happened . . . back then. Because they took so long to do it. There were two songs I was playing on, one of them was about: (starts singing) "I don't want to talk about Jesus / I Just wanna see his face." I'm playing electric piano on that. And on something else, about a mule or something, I'm not sure . . . or that was that Dr. John thing . . .
>
> But back then, there was so much going down in the, um, the drug department. When Jimmy Miller finally found out, when I told him about, "Hey man,

you guys didn't bother to give me credit for that . . . "
He and I were in business together in my solo career,
at the time, all right? So I mean years, a couple or
three years had lapsed and I'm telling you man, he
went "oh man, I knew there was something missing."

But it took so long. You know, it took them over
a year to do the recording, it was like a year and a
half. You know, they go to France, and then they're
in England, someplace else, you know, some studio
here and there. So it's a little bit of everywhere and
a lot of different people floating in and out of there.

I mentioned that Keith Richards is usually given credit
for the electric piano on "I Just Want to See His Face,"
so I asked Bobby if he overdubbed it over Keith's part,
the way Bill Plummer overdubbed bass parts later in
Los Angeles. (I thought Bobby was part of the coterie
in LA.) "Well, no, that is not when it went down," he
answered. "No, that happened in Olympic Studios . . . I
was in England." He explained that Dr. John had been
there working on his record *The Sun, Moon & Herbs*
(1971), which features contributions from Mick, Bobby
Keys, Jim Price, and many others. That greasy record
has a song called "Where Ya at Mule," which, no doubt,
is the other song to which Whitlock referred. Dr. John's
influence is clear on "I Just Want to See His Face."

I asked Whitlock, "So, that's just you on electric
piano?" Bobby answered quickly, "That would be me on

electric piano." This is contrary to every other account I have seen of the recording. One might assume that maybe there was another take of the song, but every version of the legend describes it as a spontaneous burst of inspiration.

Whitlock did not seem particularly concerned with his lack of credit on the record, nor was he eager to reminisce about the era. Responding to further inquiries as to what might be the other song that he played on, Bobby more or less dismissed it, saying, "yeah, but I don't even know. Because I haven't listened to that record since we did it. I don't sit around and listen to records, especially the ones I played on. I couldn't tell you what the name of it is. Those were some pretty hazy days, all right?"

I asked Bobby to talk a bit about Nicky Hopkins. "We were all friends. There was an opportunity for me to join the Stones but me and Eric (Clapton) were putting our band together . . . There was always a give and take (between English and American musicians)."

Al Perkins also downplayed any significance regarding the fact that British musicians were so adept at translating American music forms. After all, such music had its sources in Europe as well as Africa and other places. "I've personally enjoyed the re-wrapping process whereby American music is digested in England and presented back to America very effectively, the Stones and the Beatles being two very good examples," he said. "The Stones were great students of American blues," Perkins noted. "But along with blues must come the other forms of music from the heartland; country and gospel were major elements also."

And gospel is obviously what is on the table with "I Just Want to See His Face." The approach here starts with the raw, small-combo sound of the Staples Singers. Jimmy Miller's percussion and Charlie Watts' malleted drums sounding like a cross between African drumming and tympani, a rumble of distant thunder, provide all the atmosphere the song needs (again, Dr. John's record being a particularly good reference point). But Miller adds a tambourine for the real church feel and somehow the backing vocals from Clydie King, Jesse ("Jerry" on the record sleeve) Kirkland, and Vanetta Field (simply "Vanetta" on the credits) slip around Jagger's part as if he had charted out the whole thing beforehand. He either left the space for them intuitively, or Jimmy Miller and Los Angeles engineer Joe Zagano adeptly played around with the mute button during the mix to allow them space for a real call-and-response part.

Jagger was wise to surround himself with bona fide gospel singers to help him achieve his authentic flavor. These singers were brought in by Billy Preston. Bill Plummer overdubbed his acoustic bass part over Mick Taylor's electric bass. When he isn't playing a swinging blues part, Plummer's approach is extremely percussive, rushing high-octave runs that start and stop abruptly, adding to the atmosphere of the track. It sounds like someone is banging on an upright piano, kicking the bench, opening and shutting the keyboard cover, wood knocking and echoing in the dark. It sounds ancient or otherworldly, as if consciously made to sound like an Alan Lomax field recording, a folk relic off of Harry Smith's *Anthology of American Folk Music*, in the tradition explored on the *Basement Tapes*.

It's easy to see why Tom Waits—another fan of Dr. John—has called "I Just Want to See His Face" his favorite Stones song. The experimental spontaneity and atmospherics of the song foreshadow work by Waits, Sonic Youth, and other musicians who used room sounds and other vibe-filled textures as essential components of their recordings. "That song had a big impact on me," Waits has said of "I Just Want to See His Face." "Particularly learning how to sing in that high falsetto, the way Jagger does . . . But this is just a tree of life. This record (*Exile on Main St.*) is the watering hole. Keith Richards plays his ass off. This has the Checkerboard Lounge all over it."

Let It Loose

"Let It Loose" is one of the most beautiful songs on *Exile*, and in the Rolling Stones' canon in general. Like many great songs, it seems to take its lyrical inspiration from more than one source. After opening with a stunning Keith Richards guitar lick, an arpeggio-picked riff that warbles through a Leslie organ speaker, Mick Jagger starts in with what seems to be a dialogue: "Who's that woman on your arm . . . and I'm hip to what she'll do / give her just about a month or two." As with a few songs on *Exile*, Mick is offering caution and concern for a friend, a friend who seems suspiciously like Keith. After those opening lines, the narrator seems to switch to the other person. Perhaps it's an internal dialogue: "Bit off more than I can chew / and I knew, yeah I knew what it was leading to," and "she delivered right on time / I can't resist a corny line." It might even be Mick giving voice to Keith, perhaps a line that Keith wrote, concerned about Jagger flying off to be with Bianca and disrupting the creative flow.

Mick offers one of his most stunning performances on this song. His vocal is remarkably heartfelt, dragging out words as if each line is unloading more weight off his shoulders. On a record that features some of his most honest performances, he sounds completely guileless here, without any semblance of a mask or character, as if singing a confessional lyric from personal experience.

The "dysfunctional family" vibe that Mick Taylor and Anita Pallenberg have remarked upon was in full effect during the sessions at Nellcôte, with jealousies and concerns about the effect of outsiders—women included—on the relationships within the "gang" that was the Stones. On "Let It Loose" we seem to be privy to a brotherly conversation between Mick and Keith—though it's unlikely such words were ever actually uttered between the two Glimmer Twins. It has often been said a band is like a marriage, but in my experiences it is closer to that of siblings—rivalry very much included. Marriages and "love" relationships can, in fact, be the stabilizing forces that the individuals need to buttress them from the tempestuousness of intra-band tensions.

It is interesting that this song is somewhat buried in the middle of *Exile*; the only extra attention it receives is its placement closer to the murkiest and most enigmatic side (side three) of the album's vinyl incarnation. The production again sounds like the basement recording of *Exile*, with ghostly vocal tracks left over from the tracking, as well as off-mike whistles and hollers bleeding into open microphones, as if from other rooms, adding to the dense, layered atmosphere and live feel of the track. But it was apparently tracked at Olympic Studio in London.

The arrangement allows the ensemble to build and breathe on the 5:18 minute track. Jagger steps aside for a full minute in the middle of the song to allow for a lush and intimately quiet breakdown, featuring the backing gospel singers, a group of professional studio veterans assembled by and including Dr. John, and Tamiya Lynn (misspelled "Tammi" on the record). "What [Mick] wanted was this funk feeling, this real honest church feel," Lynn told Appleford. "He had an appreciation for black music, and he said it openly, so that was out of the way. We knew he had this affinity for the blues and where it came from. Wilson Pickett came clearly out of a church, out of a black experience. Mick came out of a respect for black experience, or black music. The greatness comes out of the spirit." The backing ensemble also includes Shirley Goodman, who had hits in the 1950s with "Let the Good Times Roll" and in the 1970s with the disco tune "Shame, Shame, Shame."

Keith's guitar lick is offered the spotlight, with Nicky Hopkins (who also has a few Mellotron "strings" lines that can be heard in the introduction) coming back in with some well-chosen country/gospel trills. Charlie slams out an elongated tom-tom fill and a typically magnificent horn chart takes it from there, building the arrangement back up to a climax. We can tell it is Bill Wyman on bass, as the part is effectively simple, made up almost completely of half-notes; no busy runs, with one note at about 2:33 that seems like a half-corrected mistake that was left in, a slur into the intended note.

Aside from some *sotto vocce* mumbling and a few shouts of encouragement, Jagger returns in earnest at the three-minute mark and seems fired up and pushed on by the ensemble. "Hide the switch and shut the light, won't you shut it?" he asks, in opposition to the album's other great gospel opus, "Shine a Light." In one of Mick's most arresting lines, he sounds deeply wounded on the impossibly drawn out "may—be your friends think I'm just a stranger / your face I'll never see no more." He vamps off the backing singers, but eventually cedes to the chorus completely, as if completely broken, letting them offer chance at salvation. It is a moment that feels divine, as the voices fade out. Listening to the vinyl edition, one is thankful for the break that is afforded with the end of the side. The listener almost needs a moment of meditation to gather one's self before the onslaught of the album's home stretch that begins with the next track, "All Down the Line."

All Down the Line

Just in case you started to get lost in the murky depths of side three and beaten down by the heavy emotion conveyed by the band on "Let It Loose," "All Down the Line" is there to slap you in the face and straighten you up, leading off side four with the same blistering hard rock assault of "Rocks Off" and "Happy," two of the other side openers. It is amazing that "All Down the Line" sounds as forceful as it does. Outtakes suggest this was a song the band really struggled with, in fits and starts, from sessions as far back as 1969, before finally reaching the state of glory it attains here on *Exile*.

The whole band is here, and it's satisfaction for the soul to hear the stellar rhythm section of Bill Wyman playing a steady bass-line groove of eighth notes inside of Charlie Watts' hard and typically crisp backbeat. The intro—played without bass—has a bit of that "Honky Tonk Women" vibe, with just a little of the tension that accompanies the wait for the rest of the band to drop in. (The album sleeve and some sources list Bill Plummer as playing acoustic bass on the track as well, but I just don't hear it anywhere.) Wyman is fiercely powerful here, content to stay pumping on the root notes until the chorus, when he slips into a James Jamerson-like Motown funk pocket with Charlie, slipping out of the choruses with very slick R&B runs (listen, for example, at 2:07–2:10). Additionally, we have that relentless early-70s-Stones percussion from Jimmy Miller, shaking it so hard that you have to shake it as well. Mick Jagger said his wish was for people to dance, not think, when listening to *Exile*.

The real star here, though, is Mick Taylor, who contributes the most distinctive instrumentation with his rapid-fire slide part. He rightfully gets one of the precious few actual guitar solos on this expansive record. The guitar tracks are very prominent in the mix, Keith leading the band with his characteristic five-string, open G-tuned chug, playing hammered suspensions slightly behind the beat. The horns again punctuate the proceedings with a Memphis punch, revving it up for all it's worth with a flurry of notes during the "oh won't you be my little baby for a while" coda. The song sports one of the most inventive horn charts of the album. Nicky Hopkins pounds away in one of his typical rock & roll barrelhouse parts, though with everything else at full-blast here, he struggles to be heard.

Jagger, also doing all he can do to be heard, has rebounded and fully recovered from the depths he plumbed on "Let It Loose." He is back to the madman yowls of side one, sounding like the wild hillbilly character of "Rip This Joint," screeching rebel yells as he barrels down country roads toward the next roadhouse. Though he needs a "sanctified girl with a sanctified mind," he is finding salvation this time as he "busts another bottle," again offering the beguiling mix of the sacred and profane that only good rock & roll can provide.

Mick sings and shouts through most of the song, as if to be heard over the mix. Here, he is just another instrument in the band, slightly above the horns and indeed almost part of the horn section, especially at the end, where his improvisations might as well be a Bobby Keys sax solo. The urgency is palpable in the timbre of his strained vocal chords, especially on lines like "keep the motor running, yeah!" (many of his lines are punctuated with similar extraneous ad-libs). He screams out of the Mick Taylor slide solo, sounding like a distorted guitar or guttural sax, rising in volume until he spits out the line "well, open up and swallow, yeah, yeah! / bust, bust, bust another bottle, yeah!" The chorus is a gratifying call-and-response between Jagger and the backing singers, including Kathi McDonald, who had been brought to the attention of the Stones by Leon Russell. She is almost an equal presence to Mick, especially on the coda. That's her solo at about 1:49. Together, they sound like the Ike and Tina Turner Revue at full speed.

Stop Breaking Down

A slinky Robert Johnson blues with Jagger on guitar and a wicked harmonica, "Stop Breaking Down" is the one of the two or three songs on *Exile* that doesn't feature Keith Richards (depending on who is playing piano on "I Just Want to See His Face"). "Keith was in charge and pulled all the strings," explained Mick Taylor. "He was always the prime mover behind the recording of *Exile* . . . Having said that, the hierarchy of power was never that clear cut—it was Mick's idea to cover Slim Harpo's 'Shake Your Hips' and Robert Johnson's 'Stop Breaking Down.'"

The track is left over from the Olympic Studios sessions, and Mick "I know I play a bad guitar" Jagger does a nice *chunka-chunk* rhythm on the electric, while Taylor shines on the slide guitar. One of the few other distinguishing elements of "Stop Breaking Down" is the rare presence of Ian Stewart, who sits in with a bluesier version of his boogie-woogie oeuvre. His rhythmic timing swings impeccably.

As with many such twelve-bar blues tracks that might otherwise be throwaway bar-band versions of the real thing, it is Jagger's commanding vocal performance that makes the song worthy of more than one or two listens. Jagger is singing live, at least for some of the track, directing the band through the same microphone (via an amplifier) he uses for his harp—thus, somewhat muddied and distorted. We can hear him shout "one more time" over the penultimate twelve bars, with hoots and howls reverberating through the old-time sounding tape echo.

If nothing else, the track further establishes the Stones' mastery of the genre that launched their career back in the suburbs of London a decade prior. And it is well placed as a filler track that gives some breathing room between the ferocious "All Down the Line" and the deep soul of "Shine a Light." Still, to my ears, "Stop Breaking Down" sounds like a rare moment when the band went back to an older track to help flesh out the record.

Shine a Light

When I first started spinning *Exile on Main St.* as a kid, "Shine a Light" was one of the first songs to hit me deeply, even though it was near the end of this long record. It made me fully aware of the influence gospel music had on not just my favorite band, the Rolling Stones, but on much of the music I loved. The first album I bought for myself (as opposed to inherited) was Stevie Wonder's *Songs in the Key of Life*, another double record with heavy gospel roots. (I guess I had a thing for sprawling records; the latter even included a four-song 45!) By the time I was out of high school, I was buying Andre Crouch records and tuning into Sunday morning broadcasts of real big-choir gospel services, the kind that made me feel something significantly more spiritual than the elaborate Catholic masses of my up-bringing. Eventually, I made the pilgrimage to Memphis to see the Reverend Al Green lead a marathon Sunday morning service in his own church, an event that has brought me as close to something God-like as anything else I have experienced. Such is the power of great music.

The Jagger/Richards track "Shine a Light" dates back to 1969 at least, when Leon Russell cut a version of it called "Get a Line on You." However, it is recorded on *Exile* as an almost solo Jagger track, with Taylor—who also plays a very groovy bass part—the only other Rolling Stones band member on the recording. It is perhaps telling that Keith makes no appearance on the track. "Shine a Light" begins with an ethereal sort of sound, a guitar being fingered, through a tape echo machine. It is the lead guitar of Mick Taylor that comes in for real at the one-minute mark. Again, we have a little extraneous noise that adds an enigmatic sense of atmosphere and texture to the multi-layered production.

Jimmy Miller is on the drums, and Billy Preston is the main man, with both an organ and a piano track. Preston, who played the awe-inspiring organ solo on "I Got the Blues" on *Sticky Fingers*, "had that gospel feel, you know, which Nicky did not have," said Andy Johns. While there is no doubt that, between the two, Preston was the more authentic gospel player, Nicky Hopkins did hone some impressive gospel chops and had made remarkable strides from his earliest days with the Stones, as is evidenced on *Exile*.

The Stones had taken stabs at the gospel form on *Beggar's Banquet* with "Salt of the Earth," and with "You Can't Always Get What You Want" on *Let It Bleed*. But both of those were bastardizations of the genre, each working on its own level, but neither would be considered close to authentic.

Let's briefly trace the development of the Stones' gospel influence. "Salt of the Earth's" vamp is gospel-like, but even the Watts St. Gospel Choir from Los Angeles can't save it from relative amateurism. But the Stones, with not only Billy Preston but also their long-time pianist Nicky Hopkins, pretty much nail a more authentic gospel sound on *Exile*, even while making it sound like something of their own. Listen, for example, to Hopkins' piano part on "Salt of the Earth," and compare it to his work on *Exile*. On the former, he seems to be locked in a jittery pattern, seemingly afraid to go out on a limb and take some chances. This is, however, symptomatic of the feel of the whole band. It is a nice try, and the song is good, but it absolutely pales in comparison to similar tracks on *Exile*. The artistic growth of the band, Hopkins included, is obvious.

"You Can't Always Get What You Want," on the next record, *Let it Bleed*, has the Jimmy Miller groove really settling in. Keith has started to play the five-string open-G-style guitar that would forever dominate the Stones sound. The rhythm is established right from the get-go, on Keith's acoustic guitar, soon after the London Bach Choir's introduction. Although the clearly no southern gospel chorus, the sound of the classical boys choir serves as an interesting combination, creating tension between the choir's straight on-the-beat phrasing and the loose gospel rhythms of Jimmy Miller on drums, leading the band through an otherwise convincing approximation of a gospel vamp. Jagger seems to sing far more freely, ad-libbing against (and seemingly spurred on by) the backing of true gospel-trained vocalists Madeline Bell, Nanette Newman, and Doris Troy (who had some hits of her own). Indeed, Jagger is screaming as the band reaches one of the most inspired climaxes in recorded pop music. Interestingly, the loose piano feel here is accomplished by Al Kooper at the keyboard, not Hopkins. And likewise, the feel of the drums is attributed to Jimmy Miller himself, who played the part after trying to demonstrate it to Charlie Watts, who ultimately deferred to Miller. Watts does the same again on "Shine a Light."

On *Exile*'s gospel-inspired tracks, Hopkins sounds as loose as he was stiff on "Salt of the Earth." He now sounds at least as good as the Al Kooper part on "You Can't Always Get What You Want." However, you would be hard-pressed to surpass Preston's playing—who at age ten was already playing with Mahalia Jackson, the superstar Queen of Gospel.

Preston lays the bedrock piano chords on the introduction of "Shine a Light," and Jagger begins his lament: "saw you stretched out in room ten-oh-nine with a smile on your face and a tear right in your eye." If there was any doubt about the subject of Jagger's lyrics on some of the album's earlier tracks, it is crystal clear on "Shine a Light." At first glance, the song is ostensibly about a party girl, but upon deeper examination and within the context of the record, this seems to be the most overt of Mick's "worried about you" *Exile* songs for Keith. As implied, these songs didn't start or end with *Exile on Main St.*: "Worried About You," "Waiting on a Friend," "Sway," "Live With Me"—there is a litany of songs that make either explicit or passing references to Keith and his relationship with Jagger. Songwriters find inspiration in emotional strife, and little causes more emotional upheaval than a creative partnership replete with continuous "sibling" rivalry. And these images on "Shine a Light" are obvious, from the blissed-out nod in the high-rise hotel room, to the "Berber jewelry," to the "drunk in the alley, baby, with your clothes all torn."

There had been a certain degree of factionalism in the Stones almost from day one, but a new era was ushered in with the making of *Exile on Main St.*, one that found Jagger and Richards most often in separate courts. "Mick was always jumping off to Paris 'cause Bianca was pregnant and having labor pains," recalled Jimmy Miller in 1977. "I remember many mornings after great nights of recording, I'd come over to Keith's for lunch. And within a few minutes of seeing him I could tell something was wrong. He'd say, 'Mick's pissed off to Paris again.' I sensed resentment in his voice because he felt we were starting to get something, and when Mick returned the magic might be gone."

Seemingly bemoaning the often seedy hangers-on in Keith's orbit, Mick sings "your late night friends will leave you in the cold gray dawn," and "just seen too many flies on you / I just can't brush 'em off," with a little Elvis Presley flourish. The record's theme of decay is in full bloom on the song, and not merely the aristo-cratic European decadence of Huysmans, but the down-town desolation of Lou Reed. Here is a dynamic in which the principals could simultaneously be jetting off to Paris and drunk in some alley with torn threads.

Mick offers a bleak perspective of his friend's future:

Angels beating all their wings in time
With smiles on their faces and a gleam right in their eye
Oh, thought I heard one sigh for you
Come on up, come on up now, come on up now

The flies have now transformed into angels. For Mick, or at least his protagonist, the sentiment is nothing less than a matter of life and death. Yet there is no urgency in his voice; the performance is one of weary acceptance and, for the most part, hopelessness. That is, until the chorus, when Mick seems to pray for (and find) the light of a higher power. The song is very much a study of dark and light, with the slow, soulful, and mournful verses and the chorus that borders on jaunty. Preston's staccato piano part and Jagger's shift in tone on the vocals are most responsible for the change in the song's mood from verse into chorus. Jimmy Miller shifts from a sparse and inventive verse beat to a steady backbeat on the chorus. The oddball rhythm section of Miller and Mick Taylor on bass shifts into an R&B groove for the chorus.

Aiding the cause significantly are the stellar backing singers, assembled in part by Preston: Clydie King, Jesse Kirkland, Joe Green, and Venetta Field. At the end of the chorus, in a section that could be labeled the re-introduction, the backing choir's vocals are also filtered through a Leslie speaker, which has the effect of blending them in with the organ. Such attention to textural detail—also illustrated in the prominence of the ghost vocals from leftover Jagger takes—adds to the haunting spacey-ness of the record.

The Stones struck a rich vein on *Exile*—adopting a sincere and authentic gospel aesthetic with ease—one that they had been after for at least four or five years. In fact, you can date the first signs of the American gospel music influence even earlier, with the guitar line from "The Last Time," which, as Keith Richards notes, "had a strong Staple Singers influence in that it came out of an old gospel song that we revamped and reworked . . . " But until they hit the target with the *Exile* songs, the Stones had merely incorporated passing elements of gospel into their overall sound, as if either too timid or too amateur to tackle the genre more directly.

There seems to be no such inhibition on *Exile*. In fact, lack of inhibition of almost any kind might be the single most winning trait of the album. On later records, however, the gospel influence seems to have dissipated faster than it took to gather. By the late 1970s records it has all but vanished. Perhaps it's this gospel component more than any other musical root that makes *Exile on Main St.* such a special record, a standout in their catalog. Though the Stones always retained soul music—which has gospel as its primary source—as a continuous and direct inspiration, it is a mystery as to why the band seemingly abandoned this true gospel sound. Their gospel exploits certainly didn't compromise their status as a rock & roll band. Indeed, it might have been the best style with which to soothe the frayed nerves of a generation. Whatever the reason, it was not likely a conscious move, but rather a natural, albeit regrettable, transition.

Soul Survivor

Lester Bangs points out that *Exile on Main St.* is largely about surviving casualties. As we have seen, these themes are easily heard on the record, which is why "Soul Survivor" might actually be the perfect way to end the whole album. I have never given much thought to this song. It is catchy enough, sure. But it almost seems to be boilerplate Stones, indicative of the formula they would exhaust for the next few records. The open-G riffing, especially as a coda over which Jagger improvises, has become prototypical Keith Richards, an MO he seems to have gotten stuck in at times. At first glance, the song seems like an anti-climatic way to end the record.

But then you take a look at the lyrics, and you have to wonder if, despite the image of this record as a big sprawl, there is not some grand design behind it all, right down to the song sequencing—I mean, beyond the obvious groupings like the mostly acoustic side two, or "the country side." No, there seems to be a certain degree of lyrical organization, from the lead-off salvo of "Rocks Off" ("heading for the overload / splattered on the dusty [dirty] road / kick me like you've kicked before / I can't even feel the pain no more") to this album closer. Coming on the heels of what seem to be Mick's pointed lyrics in "Shine a Light," he sings:

> *You've got a cut-throat crew, yeah*
> *I'm going to sink under you . . .*
>
> *. . . Yeah, yeah, it's the graveyard watch*
> *Running right on the rocks*
> *I've taken all of the knocks . . .*

. . . Yeah, when you're flying your flags
All my confidence sags
You've got me packing my bags

I'll stow away at sea
Yeah, you make me mutiny
Where you are I won't be
You're going to be the death of me, yeah

"Cut-throat crew?" "Graveyard watch?" "Mutiny?" Never mind what I said about "Shine a Light," every line in "Soul Survivor" seems to be tailor-made to articulate Jagger's feelings of alienation under the Keith regime. It is a stunning admission of humility ("my confidence sags" and "you're gonna be the death of me") until Jagger declares that he will be the "soul survivor," a clever pun for this particular strain of the sole survivor: a survivor in a soul band. Jagger's narrative voice veers sharply from that of a sainted compassionate presence to the winner of a micro-Darwinian struggle.

For all its nautical imagery, "Soul Survivor" sounds like a shot across the bow of the Good Ship Stones, with Jagger "packing [his] bags." Mick sounds like he has gone from worrying about Keith to worrying about himself. The sequencing of the album, now that we have reached the end of it, seems calculated with a perfect sense of balance and structure, at least from a lyrical standpoint. Musically, it would help if "Soul Survivor" was a rocker on par with "Happy," but its "Street Fighting Man" sort of coda is a fine way to end the record.

The pirate-movie theme is a silly, beat-through metaphor by the end of the song, but it falls in line with some of *Exile*'s other cinema references—"Dietrich movies" and the pictures in the album sleeve of a screaming Joan Crawford and movie houses. *Rolling Stone* wrote in 1977, "Aural film noir, the richly textured *Exile* is to most records what *The Big Sleep* and *Casablanca* are to made-for-TV movies." The film noir comparison is suitable; as with noir, the hero throughout much of the album is an untrustable blur between good and evil, dark and light, happy and sad. We rarely know if Mick is singing songs about himself, others in the band, women, or no one in particular.

Like some noir, the record seeps into our waking consciousness like a dream. And like a dream that we can't shake, it is free from wakeful logic. Yet its raggedness and randomness strike upon raw ephemeral truths, the kind of deep emotional revelations that can come from both dreams and nights of insomnia, resonating throughout our daylight hours. Surviving in a troubled world is perhaps the overarching lyrical concern on *Exile*. "The Stones don't have a home anymore—hence the exile," Keith said. "But they can still keep it together. Whatever people throw at us, we can still duck, improvise, overcome."

In addition to political assassinations, the mess in Vietnam, and the increasing level of violence in society, the Stones had their own personal tragedies and demons to contend with. Stanley Booth writes in *True Adventures of the Rolling Stones* "of mad Keith, and knowing that what the Stones had already done had killed one of them." He writes as if steeled against terror, an abyss he stared into at Altamont.

I have always had a hard time buying into the notion that the band's lifestyle is what killed Brian Jones, a fragile soul who by all accounts clung tenuously to life. Many people out of the public eye share similar struggles and eventually succumb. We just don't hear about them. Truth is, we all struggle. We all know friends, lovers, and family members for whom life is a fight against the shadows. *Exile on Main St.* is a masterpiece in part because, as with many classic rock & roll records, it makes us feel that we're not so alone. With the aid of *Exile*, we feel we can survive with dignity and no little style. Most of us, after all, have felt like exiles on our hometown's Main Street.

* * *

During the writing of this book, the deaths of Ronald Reagan and Ray Charles happened in quick succession. Reagan's death, in particular, unleashed a wave of sepia-stained nostalgia in America. The quick succession of their deaths resulted in strange pairings of the two men—radio stations playing sound bites of the former president's speeches over Brother Ray's genius interpretation of what should be the American national anthem, "America the Beautiful," for example. I found the coincidental pairing of these two men to be illustrative of the myth/reality dichotomy and competing worldviews that Gram Parsons pointed out wistfully to Stanley Booth in his 1969 reverie. To be sure, nostalgia, mythology, and truth often wash together and become virtually indistinguishable, but Ronald Reagan successfully sold a version of America that never really was. Ray Charles, though—blind and on his own from his early teens—was the truly self-reliant, self-made man of the American Dream. Like Parsons said, "sometimes the Mets come along and win the World Series."

When asked by *Time* magazine in 1968 to define "soul," Charles, the man generally credited with inventing soul music, answered: "It's a force that can light up a room. The force radiates from a sense of selfhood, a sense of knowing where you've been and what it means. Soul is a way of life—but it's always the hard way."

That "knowing where you've been" and radiating "selfhood" is the best description of soul music I have ever come across. Indeed, it can explain the deep emotional pull of any great music or art. But there is something about soul music in particular that digs deep into . . . well, the soul. It is not head music. It does not take multiple listens to understand. The music speaks directly to the heart. As Mick Jagger told Roy Carr, *Exile on Main St.* "is not really a thinking man's record." And the Stones have always been, above all else, a soul and R&B band.

Soul music was ubiquitous by the time I was a kid. It has always been a given, even if a lot of rock & roll deviates too far from that source for the music to matter to me anymore. With minimal fuss, soul gets to the Zen essence of what it is to be human. It's "That Feeling" that Keith Richards and Tom Waits sang about in their collaboration on the song of the same name. And the emotion comes from some deep place within, as Ray Charles notes. The first time I heard it, I knew on some base level that the songs on *Exile on Main St.* spoke to me, pulled me, tugged at me. The chord changes alone held some deeply understood truth.

In soul music, it is truly about "the singer, not the song." Listen to Aretha Franklin's stunning vocal performances on "Ain't No Way" or "I Never Loved a

Man the Way That I Love You." Listen to the pauses in the phrasing. Or recall how Ray Charles waits almost three full beats before coming in with the first word of the song "Georgia on My Mind." The ache, the shivers that arise when hearing singers like this work, is found in these spaces, in these pauses, and in the dramatically slow tempos that Ray Charles would insist on, to the bemusement of his backing musicians.

Like Robert Frank's photographs, Raymond Carver's novels, or Edward Hopper's paintings, there is a sublime beauty captured in those in-between moments. Such is the stuff of "the basic nature of our lives." If Frank's pictures are the "sad poems" Kerouac describes, then they are haikus, capturing in the specifics a more universal condition, the Buddhist acceptance that all of life is suffering. And that is precisely the same assumption of the blues, and of soul.

For fans of such performances, an inexplicable bond is formed between the listener, the performance, the song, and the singer. Waves of emotion—nostalgia, melancholy, memory—tumble over me when I hear songs like Charles' "What Would I Do?" There is nostalgia—defined as a "wistful . . . yearning"—in every pause in the singing, in certain major to minor chord changes, in manipulative Tin Pan Alley arrangements.

By way of nostalgia, we are temporal exiles. Robert Frank was criticized at the time his book was published.

Many Americans first looking at his photos mistook Frank for a surrealist, presumed to be presenting Americans with irony (despite his similar work internationally), in seemingly ordinary situations, with no apparent reason for photographic documentation. It was assumed that Frank was out to tweak noses with a vague, absurdist statement. But the Swiss photographer, as a geographic "exile," was simply looking at images Americans took for granted and *seeing* that much deeper and finding something profound.

In viewing visual art and listening to recorded music, we have the benefit of being exiled in time, looking back with new eyes on something captured in the past. We judge it via that lens. For those of us born after Frank's photos were published, their settings in a bygone era allow us to see both the surface and the substance as equally worthy of examination, if not as one and the same. Though much of the subject matter in Frank's work reflects lost relics of mid-century Americana, surely we can look at the photos without pining for the long-lost fake innocence of 50s greaser sock-hops. The notion that the 1950s was an era of shiny, positive idealism persists even after artists such as Frank have exposed another plane of subtleties, and, at times, the underbelly of the era.

In choosing Robert Frank, the Stones were cognizant of this as well; the music of the 1950s—so much of which is represented as influence on *Exile on Main St.*—was not all cartoon-like; early rock & roll music was often malevolent, raunchy, loud, raw, sexy, and sad. It was dangerous by definition: the music of the marginalized, a threat to the establishment. On *Exile*, the Stones kept that facet alive during a time when music was slipping into self-parody, big business, and bloated cultural irrelevance.

And the Stones were simultaneously mining other varied forms of mythology: the commonplace, agreed-upon notions of America, the cultural currency; the *other* America, that rural agrarian myth, that mythical America explored by Dylan and the Band; the streetwise urban hipster ("flashing knives"), and blustery swagger of Chicago bluesmen. All the while, they tapped into that musical nostalgia, ranging from older folk and country forms, to urban soul and blues, to modern hard rock—and many points in between. We are seduced by it, willingly; these are our shared myths, not lies. We want to subscribe to it all, because myths have always helped us make sense of the world, appealing to some universal, ephemeral sensation that is present in us.

Meanwhile the Stones were also selling their own press-fed mythology, as glorious, "elegantly wasted" jet-setting rock stars—the triumphs as well as the tragedies. On *Exile*, the Stones can be heard struggling with the now-cliché 60s hangover. As Lester Bangs noted: "The

Stones never bought all that brothers and sisters crap . . . when [Jagger] tried to reverse the manipulative thrust of his presence at Altamont he made himself suddenly and completely pathetic for the very first time because he was a total failure . . . "

The blank, stunned look on Jagger's face at the end of *Gimme Shelter*, after he has just viewed the footage from Altamont, testifies to the impotence and ambiguous responsibility he must have felt, implicated in the dark fallout of the late 60s. Even as he was exploiting the zeitgeist commercially, Jagger most likely never bought into the flower power ethos, and Keith certainly never did. Witness his rage, which stands in stark opposition to Jagger's weak entreaties, as Richards yells into the microphone at Altamont, "Look! Either you guys stop that shit, or you get no more music," and calls out specific perpetrators, "THAT cat, right there!" In those few moments, in which the walking dead of Keith circa '69 awakens and lets loose, we can see that he was always aware of the fact that humanity's dark side never fully abates, and he is on guard against the violent tide. The Stones had been prescient enough to warn, "a storm is threatening" in "Gimme Shelter," but were seemingly taken off guard and left powerless when the shit really did come down. As Al Maysles, along with his brother, David, co-director of *Gimme Shelter*, said in *Rolling Stone* in 1970, "Peter Fonda went looking for America. The Stones found it."

Bangs continues: "Death of Innocence in Woodstock Nation my ass, Altamont was about facing up. And the Stones were stuck in the middle of it, partly at fault, partly confused patsies from out of town who'd tried in their own mallethanded way to do something nice for a group of people toward whom, nevertheless, they almost certainly felt more contempt than anything else."

Much of *Exile on Main St.* is about coming to terms with it all. As John Perry put it, the record "has a strong claim as the first rock album to make a full *tour d'horizon*, once the dust and debris of the 1960s had settled . . . Mick and Keith were sufficiently intelligent to spot a new source of subject matter and articulate enough to set it down straight." "Kick me like you've kicked before," sings a helpless Jagger on "Rocks Off," even while his foil plays some of the most raging guitar parts of the band's history, as if it is Keith himself doing the kicking. "I can't even feel the pain no more."

And *Exile on Main St.* is a masterpiece musically because it manages to encompass a seemingly infinite amount of subtle (and not so subtle) variations on rock & roll—a form that had seemed to be severely limited to basic, guitar-driven music. Ironically, the Stones here are not aiming outside themselves, as they did with mediocre results on *Their Satanic Majesty's Request*. That record sent them scurrying home to their roots on *Beggars' Banquet*. But on *Exile* they are reaching deep *within* themselves, as men and as musicians. And, thankfully for us, a sizeable portion of who they were at the time was based on their impressive record collections: blues, gospel, folk, country, rock & roll, rockabilly, New Orleans jazz, Memphis soul, hard rock, even vocal standards all finding their way onto the album. This is not just a band at the top of its game. It is the world's best rock & roll band on top of everything, singing and playing their hearts out.

Bibliography

Books

Appleford, Steve. *Rolling Stones Rip This Joint: The Stories Behind Every Song*. New York: Thunder's Mouth Press, 2000.

Booth, Stanley. *The True Adventures of the Rolling Stones*. New York: Vintage Books, 1985.

Charone, Barbara. *Keith Richards Life as a Rolling Stone*. Garden City, NY: Doubleday, 1982.

Elliot, Martin. *The Rolling Stones Complete Recording Sessions 1963–1989*. New York: Sterling Publishing, 1990.

Frank, Robert. *The Americans.* 2nd ed. New York, Zurich, and Berlin: Salco Publishers, 1994.

Frank, Robert. *Robert Frank.* London: Thames and Hudson, 1991.

Guaralnick, Peter. *Sweet Soul Music: Rhythm and Blues and the Southern Dream of Freedom.* New York: HarperPerennial, 1986.

Mainlines, Blood Feasts, and Bad Taste: A Lester Bangs Reader. Ed. John Morthland. New York: Anchor Books, 2003.

Perry, John. *Exile on Main St., The Rolling Stones.* New York: Schirmer Books, 1999.

Sandford, Christopher. *Keith Richards: Satisfaction.* New York: Carroll & Graf Publishers, 2004 (excerpted from www.theage.com.au).

Tarlé, Dominique. *Exile: The Making of Exile on Main St.* Guildford, England: Genesis Publications Limited, 2001.

Wyman, Bill, and Richard Havers. *Rolling with the Stones.* New York: DK Publishing, 2002.

Wyman, Bill, and Ray Coleman. *Stone Alone: The Story of a Rock 'N' Roll Band.* New York: Signet, 1991.

Magazine Articles

Cook, Jno. "Robert Frank: Dissecting the American Image." *Exposure* magazine, Vol. 4, No. 1 (Spring

1986), excerpted from www.jnocook.net/frank/frank.htm.

Hodenfield, Chris. "Table Talk with Mick in Paris." *Rolling Stone*, October 28, 1971, excerpted from www.rollingstone.com.

Jones, Allan. "The Rolling Stones." *Uncut*, January 2002, pp. 45–80.

Johnstone, Nick. "Let the Tiger Out!" *Uncut*, January 2002, pp. 86–94.

Kaye, Lenny. "The Rolling Stones: Exile on Main St." *Rolling Stone*, 1972, excerpted from www.rollingstone.com.

Nelson, Paul. *Rolling Stone*, December 15, 1972, excerpted from www.superseventies.com.

Rolling Stone, December 11, 2003, excerpted from www.superseventies.com.

Simmons, Sylvie. "The Aristocats." *Mojo*, January 2002, pp. 48–62.

Newspaper Articles

"Politics Against Freedom." *New York Times*, June 5, 1970.

"California Regents Drop Communist From Faculty." Wallace Turner, *New York Times*, June 20, 1970.

"Angela Davis Is Sought in Shooting That Killed Judge on Coast." Associated Press, *New York Times*, August 16, 1970.

"F.B.I. Seizes Angela Davis in Motel Here." Linda Charlton, *New York Times*, October 14, 1970.

"The Campaign to Free Angela Davis and Ruchell Magee." Sol Stern, *New York Times*, June 27, 1971.

"Angela Davis Acquitted on All Charges." Earl Caldwell, *New York Times*, June 5, 1972.

(All *New York Times* articles taken from www.nytimes.com)

Web Sites

www.timeisonourside.com Time Is on Our Side, Ian McPherson.

www.amazon.com "Tom Waits: His Favorite Things."

www.criterionco.com "Snapshots From the Road," Georgia Bergman's commentary from DVD release of *Gimme Shelter* film for The Criterion Collection.

www.starbucks.com "Various Artists: The Rolling Stones Artist's Choice" CD.

http://www.beafifer.com/winner.htm 2003 "Songwriting and Treason," E. W. Boyle.

www.mentomusic.com

www.musicals101.com/minstrel.htm "A History of the Musical Minstrel Shows," John Kenrick.

www.theage.com.au

www.nzentgraf.de *The Complete Works Website: The Rolling Stones Database*, Nico Zentgraf.

www.barryrudolph.com "Rod Stewart," Barry Rudolph.

www.allmusic.com

Films

Cocksucker Blues (Robert Frank and Daniel Seymour, 1972)

Gimme Shelter (Albert Maysles, David Maysles, and Charlotte Zwerin, 1970)